THE MICROWAVE
CHINESE COOKBOOK

湘波食谱

THE MICROWAVE CHINESE COOKBOOK

LILLIAN CHEN
EDITH NOBILE

VNR VAN NOSTRAND REINHOLD COMPANY
NEW YORK CINCINNATI TORONTO LONDON MELBOURNE

Designed by Karolina Harris
Photography by David Knox/Ann Arbor Photographic, Inc.
Step-by-step drawings by Joanne Newman
Decorative drawings from *Chinese Folk Designs,* published by Dover Publications, Inc.

Published by Van Nostrand Reinhold Company
135 West 50th Street
New York, NY 10020

Van Nostrand Reinhold Limited
1410 Birchmount Road
Scarborough, Ontario M1P 2E7, Canada

Van Nostrand Reinhold Australia Pty. Ltd.
17 Queen Street
Mitcham, Victoria 3132, Australia

Van Nostrand Reinhold Company Limited
Molly Millars Lane
Wokingham, Berkshire, England

16 15 14 13 12 11 10 9 8 7 6 5 4 3 2

Library of Congress Cataloging in Publication Data

Chen, Lillian.
　The microwave Chinese cookbook.

　Includes index.
　1. Cookery, Chinese.　2. Cookery, Microwave.
I. Nobile, Edith.　II. Title.
TX724.5.C5C5433　　1981　　　　641.5951　　　　81-4704
ISBN 0-442-22096-0　　　　　　　　　　　　　AACR2

CONTENTS

PREFACE

Lillian Chen, XIE Meng-Yuan, recalls from her childhood in Beijing (Peking) the exciting family trips to historical sights and famous restaurants in other regions of China. When a teenager, she left her family with mixed feelings of regret and anticipation to attend college in the United States. The separation was assumed to be temporary. During her student years she married Kan, a graduate engineering student at the Massachusetts Institute of Technology. Lillian earned a degree in home economics and dietetics. They managed to travel in several countries while bringing up four children. For many years, Lillian has enjoyed sharing her knowledge of Chinese culture, language, and cooking through her numerous courses and tutoring. In 1977, after a twenty-nine year separation, Lillian returned to the People's Republic of China and was reunited with her mother and five sisters and brothers for a month. She collected recipes from famous chefs and restaurants in China and Hong Kong, combining two lifelong interests, travel and foods.

It is a curious coincidence that Edith Nobile was a research chemist in metallurgy at M.I.T. when Kan was there. She has a degree in chemistry and biology. Edith and Lillian met for the first time a few years ago in Ann Arbor, Michigan, where both families live. Edith pursued her career for many years in universities and industries. In tiny Boston apartments, a New Jersey country farmhouse, and sandy Cape Cod summer cottages she indulged her avocation: French, Italian, and other international cooking. She remembers fondly her mother's talents with various cuisines, which gave Edith an appreciation for good food prepared and served with elegance. She and her husband, Vincent, enjoyed a decade of exploring the delights of New York restaurants from the imposing uptown establishments to the modest Greenwich Village cafés. In the years that followed, they shared their enthusiasm for science and foods with three growing children.

Edith and Lillian assessed their skills, technical experience, and mutual interests. Since they entertain frequently, they recognized the advantages of a microwave cookbook for the busy host and hostess who like Chinese food. They spent two years experimenting, testing, and developing Chinese recipes for the microwave oven.

The authors hope that the brief introductions to the chapters will contribute to the current interest in Chinese traditions, history, and customs. They are convinced that microwave cooking can be a rewarding experience.

ACKNOWLEDGMENTS

We dedicate this book to our families, who have given us continuing encouragement in this endeavor. They have made this an enjoyable project for us by actively participating and assisting in our experiments.

Our special thanks go to Kathy Nobile for her generous assistance and support. We are also deeply indebted to Dr. Tai Chen-To for his accomplished calligraphy on the title page and the chapter headings.

Acknowledgments are also due to David Knox for his artful photography and Joanne Newman for her illustrations.

INTRODUCTION

This book offers a new and rapid way to cook classic Chinese dishes. With our recipes you can have typical stir-fried, steamed, fried, and simmered foods using only the microwave oven. Cooking times and number of servings have been noted in the recipes for your convenience.

We want to dispel the mystique about Chinese cooking and have provided brief uncomplicated preparations in which we clearly state the desired weight, thickness, or shape of ingredients. In a few recipes, we call for a shallow angle or slant slicing of fibrous vegetables and tough cuts of meat to increase tenderness. For utensils, you need a few sharp knives or a cleaver, spoons, and forks or chopsticks. The Chinese are practical about cooking and you, too, should use whatever tools you have that do the job.

Chinese microwave cooking is economical. You can make savory dishes using small quantities of meat with the addition of vegetables and good seasonings. Inexpensive cuts of meat are often preferred for their superior flavor or texture, and smaller quantities of expensive ingredients are used. Foods can be cooked in low-cost ovenproof glass dishes with commercial plastic wrap for covers. We have described our book as wokless Chinese cooking since no specialized equipment is needed.

Nutritionally, many Chinese dishes are low in fat and our recipes call for even less oil in stir frying than do conventional ones.

The list of essential ingredients is short and readily available: vegetable oil, dry sherry, soy sauce, garlic, ginger root, and scallions (green onions). Desirable staples are cayenne pepper, chili powder, hoisin sauce, oyster sauce, fermented black beans, dried Chinese mushrooms, commercial noodles, and noodle wrappers. In Chapter 10, we have included recipes for several commercial Chinese products in case you cannot find them in stores or simply prefer to make them from "scratch."

If you want to serve more people than the recipes provide for, prepare several batches and cook them in succession rather than cooking a single large batch. Many other factors besides quantity affect foods cooked by microwaves: they include temperature of the food and arrangement in the dish, food shape, and density (thin slices cook faster than cubes, and vegetables cook faster than meat). In Chapter 13 we have explained these factors in detail so that you can have successful results with the microwave oven. We recommend that you read this section carefully.

THE MICROWAVE
CHINESE COOKBOOK

伴碟

1 · APPETIZERS

Picture a scene in the beautiful lake city of Hangchow during the Sung dynasty with throngs of people crowding the Imperial Way. Here restaurants, tea and wine houses, specialty food shops, and open stands competed for customers. Elegant restaurants catered to wealthy officials and merchants while street vendors supplied simple tasty food to the poor. The private rooms of expensive restaurants were sumptuously furnished with paintings, silver, delicate porcelains, plants, and glamorous hostesses, all designed to please the sophisticated clientele. Royalty, despite their talented kitchen staffs, patronized those that boasted notable specialties. Even the emperor occasionally presided over a catered banquet in one of his island palaces on the great West Lake.

Teahouses offered delicious *dim sum,* which translates as dot-heart or touch-the-heart. Hearty snacks, steamed and fried stuffed dumplings, baked buns and cakes, pickled and preserved eggs, fish, and vegetables were served from morning to night. The Cantonese used the expression ''going to drink tea'' when visiting the teahouses, which meant eating snacks, drinking tea, meeting friends, and exchanging news and gossip. These shops were centers of social and business activities. The more boisterous patrons of the winehouses gathered to relish their favorite foods cooked to order by the owners. Modest shops specialized in noodle dishes, soups, or temple foods, which were vegetarian dishes popularized by Buddhists. Humble shops, nothing more than stalls and lightly roofed open sheds, provided cheap quick meals and snacks to take home. In the streets, vendors served plain boiled noodles in bowls, which they rinsed and reused. In vivid contrast to this informality, the elite during the Sung period adopted the use of dining tables and chairs, which until then had been a novelty.

Among the recipes in this chapter, we have included Shao Mai and Chiao Tze (stuffed dumplings), Bao Tze (stuffed buns), and fried Won Ton. We found that twelve Shao Mai but only nine Bao Tze cooked properly with the microwave method. The density and spacing of the foods affect the amounts that can be successfully prepared. We found that twenty Won Ton can be cooked conveniently in twenty-six minutes but more batches would be laborious. You can freeze unused wrappers for future use. Bao Tze, Chiao Tze, Pearl Meatballs, Shao Mai, Soy Eggs, and Stuffed Mushrooms can also be served as main dishes. In either event, varying amounts are in keeping with the Chinese custom of serving many dishes that diners can share but not always equally.

牛肉包子
BEEF BAO TZE (STUFFED BUNS)

Servings: 4 to 6   Cooking time: 5 minutes

1 package ready-to-bake refrigerated biscuits
Beef stuffing (see below)
Waxed paper, cut in 9 2-inch squares
1 tablespoon water
3 large cabbage leaves (thin outer leaves)
Soy sauce dip (see below)

Open package of biscuits and let stand 20 minutes. Meanwhile, prepare stuffing as described.

Roll out 9 biscuits into 3-inch circles on lightly floured surface. Place 1 heaping tablespoon stuffing in center of each circle, wrap dough around stuffing, overlapping each fold, and twist top to seal as shown. Place buns on waxed paper squares and let stand 10 minutes.

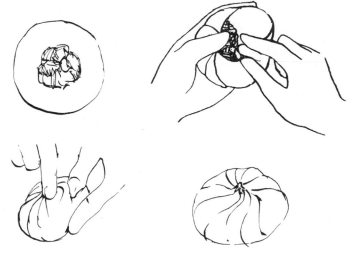

Add water to 10-inch heatproof round dish and line with single layer of cabbage leaves. Space buns around outer edge so that they do not touch. Cover with plastic wrap, leaving small vent. Cook on High 2 minutes. Give dish a quarter turn. Cook on High 3 minutes more and let stand covered 5 minutes. Peel paper from bottoms and serve buns with dip. Buns have white thick tender tops, fragrant moist fillings, and thin moist bottoms.

BEEF STUFFING
½ pound ground beef (about 1 cup)
½ cup chopped water chestnuts
2 tablespoons diced yellow onion
2 teaspoons minced ginger root
1 tablespoon dry sherry
1 tablespoon soy sauce
1½ teaspoons curry powder
⅛ teaspoon salt

Combine beef, chestnuts, onion, ginger, and mix well. Add rest of ingredients and mix well.

SOY SAUCE DIP
4 tablespoons soy sauce
2 tablespoons vinegar
¼ teaspoon sesame oil (optional)
Dash Tabasco sauce (optional)

Combine all ingredients, mix well, and serve in small bowl.

TIPS
Buns can be served with Cooked Soy Dip (page 114).

Bao Tze can be served as a main dish.

Do not use flaky type biscuits. Do not use thick inner cabbage leaves, which have too much moisture and will make bottoms soggy instead of moist.

Only nine buns cook properly, probably because of the dense stuffing and lighter dough wrapping, and the limits of space even in a large dish. Enough space must be left between buns to allow for expansion and rising of biscuit dough.

猪肉包子
PORK BAO TZE (STUFFED BUNS)

Servings: 4 to 6   Cooking time: 5 minutes

1 package ready-to-bake refrigerated biscuits
Pork stuffing (see below)
Waxed paper, cut in 9 2-inch squares
1 tablespoon water
3 large cabbage leaves (thin outer leaves)
Soy sauce dip (see page 17)

Follow directions for preparing Beef Bao Tze (page 16), substituting pork stuffing. Serve with Soy Sauce Dip (page 17).

PORK STUFFING
½ pound ground pork
½ cup finely chopped cabbage
1 tablespoon soy sauce
2 teaspoons finely chopped scallions
2 teaspoons dry sherry
½ teaspoon sugar
½ teaspoon minced ginger root
¼ teaspoon sesame oil

Combine all ingredients and mix well.

餃子
CHIAO TZE (STUFFED DUMPLINGS)

Servings: 50 dumplings   Cooking time: 3 minutes per batch of 10 dumplings

1 pound package wrappers (thin 2½- to 3-inch rounds of dough)
Pork stuffing (see below)
¼ teaspoon vegetable oil
¼ cup water

Lay out 10 wrappers at a time and moisten edges with water. Place 1 heaping teaspoon stuffing in center of each circle. Press edges together at the middle, leaving ends open. Starting at one open end, make a few pleats to the middle. Repeat pleating on other side. Press pleated edges to seal. Lightly press each bottom flat. Shape finished dumplings into shallow crescents as shown.

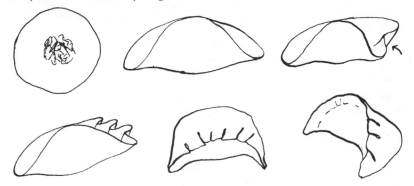

Coat a 10-inch heatproof pie plate with oil. Add water to plate. Space 10 dumplings around outer edge of dish so that they do not touch. Cover with plastic wrap. Do not vent. Cook on High 2 minutes. Give dish a quarter turn. Cook on High 1 minute. Remove plastic wrap. Turn dumplings over. Let stand 2 to 3 minutes.

PORK STUFFING

1½ cups finely chopped American cabbage
½ pound lean ground pork
2 tablespoons chopped scallions
2 tablespoons dry sherry
2 tablespoons soy sauce
1 tablespoon sesame oil
1 teaspoon minced ginger root
¼ teaspoon salt

Mix ingredients well together.

TIPS

The thin round wrappers for this dish are commonly sold as "Gyoza" wrappers, usually about 50 sheets to a pound.

To store unused wrappers, cover tightly with plastic wrap, then aluminum foil. They will keep a few days refrigerated and several weeks when frozen.

For more than 10 dumplings, cook in batches of 10.

Dumplings may be served with Soy and Vinegar Dip (page 116) or Cooked Soy Dip (page 114).

SOY SAUCE EGGS

Servings: 4 to 6   Cooking time: 3 minutes

6 large eggs, hardcooked
1 cup soy sauce
2 teaspoons minced ginger root
½ teaspoon sugar
½ teaspoon salt

Peel eggs and cut four ½-inch slits into white on opposite sides of each egg. Do not penetrate yolk.

Combine remaining ingredients for marinade in small, heatproof bowl and heat on High 1 to 2 minutes, or until boiling. Add hardcooked eggs to hot marinade. Cover, leaving small vent. Heat on High 1 minute. Turn eggs over and let stand in marinade for 1 minute, in or out of oven. Remove eggs from marinade and let cool to room temperature.

Eggs will be a golden brown color and have a delicate, spicy exterior. They may be served whole or quartered.

TIPS
Soy eggs quartered make a colorful edible garnish.

Eggs can be hardcooked in microwave oven (see page 91).

Eggs warmed to room temperature are less likely to crack during hardcooking. Place cold eggs in tepid water for a few minutes to warm before hardcooking.

When hardcooked eggs are placed in cold water immediately after cooking, the shells can be removed easily and will not adhere to the surface of the eggs.

茶葉蛋
TEA EGGS

Servings: 4 to 6   Cooking time: 13½ minutes

6 eggs, hardcooked in shell
2 cups water
8 bags or 5 tablespoons black tea
3 tablespoons soy sauce
2 teaspoons five-spice powder
1 teaspoon salt

Tap shells very lightly all over to form hairline cracks. Try not to break through the shell. Do not remove shells.

Combine remaining ingredients for marinade in 1-quart heat-proof bowl. Put eggs in marinade. Cover bowl, leaving small vent. Heat on High 3½ minutes. Heat on Low 10 minutes.

Let eggs cool in marinade to room temperature. Refrigerate eggs in marinade 10 to 12 hours.

Remove eggs from marinade and refrigerate. Peel eggs just before serving. Peeled eggs have a beautifully marbled appearance and subtle spicy flavor.

TIPS
Eggs can be hardcooked in microwave oven (see page 91).

If the shells are broken through, the peeled tea eggs will have solid brown areas. These brown spots do not affect the flavor or texture of the tea eggs but detract from the desired overall marbleized appearance.

PEARL MEATBALLS

Servings: 4 to 6   Cooking time: 9 minutes

½ cup plus 3 tablespoons water
⅜ teaspoon salt
¼ cup glutinous rice
½ pound ground pork
1 tablespoon dry sherry
1 tablespoon soy sauce
2 tablespoons chopped scallions
1 teaspoon minced ginger root
¼ teaspoon sesame oil
3 large cabbage leaves (thin outer leaves only)

Add ½ cup water and ¼ teaspoon salt to rice in 2-cup heatproof bowl. Cook on High 3 minutes. Let stand 10 minutes. Drain rice and wash in cold water. Spread out on plate.

Combine pork, sherry, and soy sauce, scallions, ginger root, sesame oil, and remaining ⅛ teaspoon salt, and mix well. Divide mixture into 12 portions and lightly form into balls. Roll each ball in rice until coated.

To a 10-inch or larger round heatproof dish add remaining 3 tablespoons water. Line with cabbage leaves. Arrange meatballs in dish so they do not touch. Leave center open. Cover tightly and cook on High 3 minutes. Give dish a quarter turn. Cook on High 3 minutes more. Let stand 10 minutes.

TIPS

Glutinous rice is also called sweet rice. If not available, short grain rice may be substituted.

Rice is partially cooked before coating meatballs. Final cooking of rice is completed by cooking together with the meatballs.

煨鮮菇
SOY-MARINATED MUSHROOMS

Servings: 4 to 6   Cooking time: 3 minutes

1 pound fresh mushrooms, halved (if large, cut in 3 pieces)
½ cup vegetable oil
¼ cup soy sauce
1 teaspoon salt

In large heatproof bowl mix mushrooms and oil. Add soy sauce and salt and mix.

Cook on High 2 minutes. Give dish a quarter turn. Stir. Cook on High 1 minute more.

Remove mushrooms from oil with slotted spoon. Let stand a few minutes. Serve hot or cold.

TIP
Mushrooms should have firm texture.

冬菇釀肉

STUFFED CHINESE MUSHROOMS

Servings: 4 to 6   Cooking time: 8 minutes

24 dried Chinese mushrooms
½ pound ground pork
4 to 6 medium size raw shrimp, minced
¼ cup water chestnuts, diced small
2 tablespoons soy sauce
1 tablespoon chopped scallions
1 teaspoon dry sherry
½ teaspoon minced ginger root
¼ teaspoon sesame oil
¼ teaspoon sugar
1 egg, unbeaten
Parsley for garnish (optional)

Rinse mushrooms, then soak in hot water until soft, 20 to 30 minutes, drain. Save liquid for future use in soup or sauce. Remove hard stems and discard.

Combine pork, shrimp, chestnuts, soy sauce, scallions, sherry, ginger root, sesame oil, sugar, and egg, and mix well. Divide mixture into 24 portions. Heap a portion on each mushroom cap. Arrange mushrooms in heatproof dish, leaving center open. Cook on High 4 minutes. Give dish a quarter turn. Cook on High 4 minutes more. Let stand 2 minutes, inside or outside oven.

TIPS
Dried Chinese mushrooms may be softened quickly in microwave oven. In this recipe the longer process is recommended, but if you wish to try the microwave method, follow instructions given in recipe for Stuffed Fresh Mushrooms (page 25).

Always rinse dried mushrooms before soaking to remove small particles that can cause too much foaming when they are heated in water and result in overflow from the bowl.

鮮菇釀肉

STUFFED FRESH MUSHROOMS

Servings: 4 to 6   Cooking time: 10 minutes

1 pound fresh mushrooms
3 to 4 dried Chinese mushrooms
1 pound ground pork
1 egg, unbeaten
2 tablespoons soy sauce
2 tablespoons chopped scallions
1 tablespoon dry sherry
1 teaspoon minced ginger root
¼ teaspoon salt

Wash and dry fresh mushrooms, reserving stems. To prepare stuffing, rinse dried Chinese mushrooms and place in 1-quart heatproof measure with 1 cup warm water. Cover with plastic wrap, leaving small vent. Heat on High 4 minutes. Let stand 5 minutes, in or out of oven. Remove hard stems and discard. Chop and combine with pork, egg, soy sauce, scallions, sherry, ginger, salt, and reserved fresh mushroom stems, chopped. Mix well.

Heap into fresh mushroom caps.

Arrange in heatproof dish, leaving center open. Cook on High 3 minutes. Give dish a quarter turn. Cook on High 3 minutes more.

TIP
Always rinse dried mushrooms before soaking to remove small particles that can cause too much foaming when they are heated in water and result in overflow from the bowl.

四川花生

BLANCHED SZECHUAN PEANUTS

Servings: 4 to 6   Cooking time: 5 minutes

2 teaspoons ground star anise
1½ teaspoons whole Szechuan peppercorns
1 teaspoon salt
1 tablespoon water
2 cups blanched raw peanuts

Mix anise, peppercorns, and salt with water. Add spice mixture to peanuts and stir well. Spread peanuts evenly in large heatproof dish, leaving center open.

Cook on High 3 minutes. Give dish a quarter turn. Cook on High 2 minutes more. Let cool to room temperature.

TIP
Szechuan peanuts may be stored in tightly covered container for several weeks.

香酥花生米

SPICED SZECHUAN PEANUTS

Servings: 4 to 6   Cooking time: 8 minutes

2 teaspoons five-spice powder
1 teaspoon salt
1 tablespoon water
2 cups raw, unblanched peanuts
1 teaspoon sesame oil

Mix spice powder and salt with water. Add mixture to peanuts and stir well. Sprinkle oil over peanuts. Mix and toss well. Spread evenly in heatproof dish, leaving center open.

Cook on High 3 minutes. Stir well. Spread evenly, leaving center open. Cook on High 5 minutes more. Allow to cool to room temperature.

TIP
Spiced peanuts may be stored in tightly covered container for several weeks.

炸餛飩
FRIED WON TON

Servings: 4 to 6   Cooking time: 26 minutes

2 cups vegetable oil
2 teaspoons salt
20 won ton wrappers
1 teaspoon flour mixed with 1 tablespoon water
Stuffing (see below)

Put oil and salt into 2-quart heatproof bowl and cover loosely with paper plate. Heat on High 13 minutes, or until temperature reaches 350 to 360 degrees.

While oil heats, prepare stuffed won ton. Lay out a few wrappers at a time, and moisten borders of each wrapper with flour-water mixture.

Place ½ teaspoon stuffing in center. Fold into triangle and seal edges. Bring bottom corners to meet. Moisten and seal as shown.

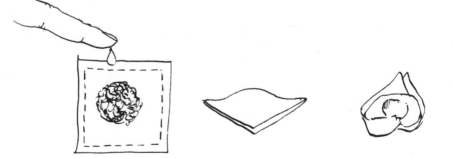

Place 10 stuffed won ton, one at a time, in heated oil, dipping each one under oil as added. Cover bowl with paper plate. Cook on High 1½ minutes. Turn each won ton over in oil to cook a few seconds. Remove from oil with slotted spoon and drain on paper towels. Cover bowl with paper plate, reheat oil on High 6 minutes, or until temperature reaches 350 degrees. Repeat frying for second batch.

STUFFING
2 dried Chinese mushrooms
¼ pound ground pork
2 tablespoons chopped raw, shelled, deveined shrimp
1 tablespoon chopped scallion
1 tablespoon dry sherry
1 tablespoon soy sauce
1 teaspoon minced ginger root
½ teaspoon salt
¼ teaspoon sesame oil

Rinse mushrooms and place in 1-quart heatproof measure with 1 cup warm water. Cover with plastic wrap, leaving small vent. Heat on High 4 minutes. Let stand 5 minutes, in or out of oven. Remove hard stems and discard. Chop mushrooms and combine with remaining stuffing ingredients. Mix well.

TIPS
Oil, if refrigerated to avoid rancidity, can be reused for frying more won ton or saved for other deep frying dishes.

Always rinse dried mushrooms before soaking to remove small particles that can cause too much foaming when they are heated in water and result in overflow from the bowl.

Keep wrappers covered until stuffed. They dry out rapidly.

BEEF SHAO MAI

Servings: 4 to 6   Cooking time: 5 minutes

12 won ton wrappers
Beef stuffing (see below)
2 tablespoons water
3 large cabbage leaves (thin outer leaves only)

Cut off the corners of each wrapper, removing triangles about ½ inch at the base. Brush with water completely one side of each wrapper. On moist surface of wrapper place 1 heaping tablespoon stuffing. Gather up wrapper to form a fluted cup around stuffing, leaving top open. Lightly press sides toward center so that stuffing mounds slightly. Brush outside of dumpling completely with water. Lightly press bottom on flat surface so that dumpling will remain upright. Make 12 dumplings, following the wrapping instructions shown.

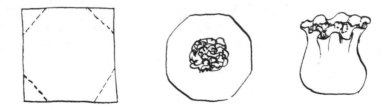

To a large round heatproof dish add 2 tablespoons water. Line dish with single layer of cabbage leaves. Space dumplings on cabbage leaves around outer sides of dish so they are not touching. Cover dish tightly with plastic wrap. Cook on High 3 minutes. Give dish a quarter turn. Cook on High 2 minutes more.

Let dumplings stand, covered, about 5 minutes. Wrappers should be tender and stuffing moist.

BEEF STUFFING
½ pound ground beef
½ cup chopped water chestnuts
2 tablespoons chopped yellow onions
1 tablespoon black bean chili sauce

1 tablespoon dry sherry
2 teaspoons soy sauce
1 thin slice ginger root, minced
¼ teaspoon sugar

Combine ingredients and mix well.

TIPS
Corners cut from wrappers may be added to soup.

Brushing wrappers with water prevents toughening and drying.

Black bean chili sauce may be replaced by a mixture of 1 minced garlic clove, 4 drops or more Tabasco sauce, and 1 tablespoon chopped salted black beans.

猪 肉 烧 賣
PORK SHAO MAI

Servings: 4 to 6   Cooking time: 5 minutes

12 won ton wrappers
Pork stuffing (see below)
2 tablespoons water
3 large cabbage leaves (thin outer leaves only)

Follow directions for Beef Shao Mai (page 30), substituting pork stuffing.

PORK STUFFING
½ pound ground pork
¼ cup finely chopped cabbage
1 tablespoon chopped scallions
1 tablespoon soy sauce
1 tablespoon dry sherry
1 teaspoon minced ginger root
¼ teaspoon sesame oil

Combine all ingredients and mix well.

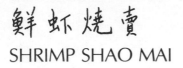

SHRIMP SHAO MAI

Servings: 4 to 6   Cooking time: 9 minutes

10 won ton wrappers
Shrimp stuffing (see below)
1 tablespoon water
3 large cabbage leaves (thin outer leaves)

Follow directions for Beef Shao Mai (page 30), substituting shrimp stuffing.

SHRIMP STUFFING
2 to 3 dried Chinese mushrooms
½ pound raw shrimp, shelled, deveined, and chopped
¼ cup chopped bamboo shoots
1 tablespoon dry sherry
1 teaspoon soy sauce
½ teaspoon vegetable oil
½ teaspoon minced garlic clove
¼ teaspoon salt

Rinse mushrooms and place in 1-quart heatproof measure with 1 cup warm water. Cover with plastic wrap, leaving small vent. Heat on High 4 minutes. Let stand 5 minutes, in or out of oven. Remove hard stems and discard. Chop mushrooms and combine with other stuffing ingredients. Mix well together.

TIPS
Corners cut from wrappers may be added to soup.

Brushing wrappers with water prevents toughening and drying.

Always rinse dried mushrooms before soaking to remove small particles that can cause too much foaming when they are heated in water and result in overflow from the bowl.

Lion's Head Dumplings and Long Grain Rice at a portal of the ancient Manchurian palace at Shenyang.

Spicy Steamed Mussels, Succulent Shrimp with Snow Peas, and Carrots with Garlic and Black Beans on the banks of the Li River in Guangsi Autonomous Region.

Almond Float set against statues of Buddha carved in the rocks near Hangchow.

Stuffed Cucumbers with Pork, Spiced Eggs in Meat Sauce, and Asparagus Salad, with the Chu Bridge of Nanjing visible in the background.

汤 羹

2 · SOUP

In ancient China, *keng*, a hearty stew of vegetables and grains was popular with rulers and subjects alike. Keng with meat was a luxury of the wealthy. Congee, a rice gruel, was sometimes flavored with soy sauce and ginger. Eggs, meat, or fruit were often added to the soup and eaten for breakfast, lunch, and as a late-night snack. A famous congee called Seven-Treasure-Five-Taste commemorated a Buddhist holiday. There is a legend about a Hangchow woman who prepared a fish soup that greatly pleased a visiting emperor. His approval made her so illustrious that she was immortalized in poetry. Present-day restaurants in that city claim to serve a soup made from the original recipe.

During the Tang dynasty, a carp soup with bean relish and wine sediment was offered as tribute to the emperor. The affluent evoked the flattery of guests with exotic soups of bears' paws, birds' nests, and sharks' fins. Actually, these costly ingredients did not greatly enrich the flavor of the broth. Chinese soups are often chicken stock and bits of meat, eggs, tofu (bean curd), vegetables, and leftovers. A special banquet dish, Winter Melon Soup, is cooked in a large hollowed-out green melon. The soup and some of the tender inner melon flesh is ladled directly from the melon into individual bowls.

A communal bowl of soup accompanies a main Chinese meal rather than tea. An ancient scholar offered the advice that soup should not be seasoned once served and should be savored slowly.

蛋花湯
EGG FLOWER SOUP

Servings: 4 to 6   Cooking time: 8 minutes

4 cups chicken broth, homemade or canned
2 tablespoons cornstarch mixed with 3 tablespoons water
2 eggs, well beaten
Salt to taste
¼ teaspoon white pepper
1 tablespoon chopped scallion

Pour chicken broth into heatproof 1½- or 2-quart bowl, cover, leaving small vent. Heat on High 7 to 9 minutes, or until boiling.

Stir in cornstarch mixture, re-cover, leaving small vent. Heat on High 1 to 3 minutes, or until boiling.

Slowly pour in beaten eggs while stirring gently in a circular pattern to form thin threads of cooked egg. Heat of broth is enough to cook eggs.

Taste for salt, add pepper and scallion, and serve.

TIP
Canned broth tends to be saltier than homemade, so taste before adding salt.

酸辣湯
SOUR-AND-HOT SOUP

Servings: 4 to 6   Cooking time: 18 minutes

6 dried Chinese mushrooms
1 small peeled carrot
Pinch of salt
Pinch of pepper
2 ounces shredded pork (about ¼ cup)
1 teaspoon cornstarch
4 ounces boiled ham (about ½ cup)

4 cups chicken broth, homemade or canned
1 5-ounce can bamboo shoots cut in thin strips
½ cup tofu (bean curd), cut in strips 1 inch long by ½ inch thick
Sauce (see below)
3 eggs, well beaten

Rinse mushrooms, drain, and put into 1-quart measure with 1 cup warm water. Cover with plastic wrap, leaving small vent, and heat on High 4 minutes. Let stand 5 minutes, in or out of oven. Remove hard stems and discard. Cut mushrooms into thin strips and reserve.

Wrap carrot in plastic wrap and partially cook on High 1 minute. Cut into thin 2-inch strips and reserve. Add salt and pepper to pork and mix. Add cornstarch, mix, and reserve.

Cut ham into thin 2-inch-long strips and reserve. Put chicken broth into 1½- or 2-quart heatproof bowl and cover, leaving small vent. Heat to boil on High 9 minutes, then add mushrooms, carrots, pork, ham, bamboo shoots, and tofu. Cover bowl, leaving small vent, and reheat to boil on High 3 to 4 minutes. Stir sauce into soup and cover, leaving small vent. Reheat to boil on High 1 minute.

Remove from oven and slowly pour in beaten eggs while stirring gently in a circular pattern to form thin threads of cooked egg. Heat of broth is enough to cook eggs. Serve at once in warmed bowls.

SAUCE
5 tablespoons water
3 tablespoons cornstarch
2 tablespoons soy sauce
2 tablespoons cider or white vinegar
1½ teaspoons salt (omit if canned chicken broth used)
½ teaspoon pepper

Mix ingredients together.

菠菜豆腐湯

SPINACH AND TOFU SOUP

Servings: 4 to 6   Cooking time: 10 minutes

4 cups beef broth, homemade or canned
1 slice ginger root, ¼ inch thick
½ pound spinach, washed, drained, stems removed
1 pound tofu (bean curd), cut in 1-inch squares, ¼ inch thick
Salt to taste

Pour beef broth into 1½- or 2-quart heatproof bowl. Add ginger slice. Cover, leaving small vent, and cook on High 7 to 9 minutes, or until boiling.

Add spinach and tofu. Re-cover, leaving small vent, and cook on High 3 minutes more, or until boiling. Salt to taste.

TIPS
Bouillon cubes may be substituted for broth. Canned broth and bouillon tend to be salty.

Ginger slice may be discarded before adding the vegetables, or retained through remainder of preparation of soup.

餛飩湯

WON TON SOUP

Servings: 4 to 6   Cooking time: 25 minutes

5 cups water
½ teaspoon salt
1 teaspoon vegetable oil
4 to 6 cups chicken broth, homemade or canned
30 won ton (see below), approximately
2 teaspoons chopped scallions, for garnish

Put water, salt, and oil in a 2-quart heatproof bowl. Cover with plastic wrap, leaving small vent, and heat on High 9 to 11 minutes, or until boiling.

While water heats, prepare won ton.

WON TON

10 ounces frozen chopped spinach, defrosted
½ pound ground pork
½ teaspoon salt
1 teaspoon dry sherry
1 teaspoon soy sauce
½ teaspoon sugar
½ teaspoon sesame oil
½ teaspoon minced ginger root
½ pound won ton wrappers, about 30
1 teaspoon flour mixed with 1 teaspoon water

To defrost spinach, place in heatproof dish and heat on Low 5 minutes. Squeeze out as much liquid as possible. Combine spinach with pork, salt, sherry, soy sauce, sugar, sesame oil, and ginger, and mix well.

Lay out a few won ton wrappers at a time and moisten edges of each wrapper on one side with flour-water mixture. Place 1 teaspoon stuffing in center. Fold into triangle and seal edges. Bring bottom corners to meet, moisten, seal (see recipe for Fried Won Ton, page 28).

Add won ton to boiling water. Cover, leaving small vent. Cook on High 4 minutes. Remove with slotted spoon. Reserve.

Place chicken broth in 2-quart heatproof bowl. Cover with plastic wrap, leaving small vent, and heat on High for 7 to 9 minutes until warm. Add reserved won ton to soup. Garnish with scallions.

TIPS
Canned chicken broth tends to be salty.

Keep wrappers covered until stuffed. They dry out rapidly.

粟米羹
VELVET CORN SOUP

Servings: 4 to 6   Cooking time: 8½ minutes

3 cups chicken broth, homemade or canned
1 cup canned cream-style corn
2 tablespoons cornstarch mixed with 1 tablespoon water
1 egg, slightly beaten
Cilantro (Chinese parsley) for garnish (optional)

Mix together chicken broth and corn in heatproof bowl. Cover, leaving small vent, and cook on High 6 minutes or until boiling. Add cornstarch mixture and stir well. Re-cover, leaving small vent, and cook on High 2½ minutes more or until boiling. Slowly stir in egg. Let stand 5 minutes. Garnish with cilantro, if desired.

牛 肉

3 · BEEF

When the Mongols occupied China, they brought with them their Muhammadan religion and customs. These fierce nomadic tribes relied for food on large herds of sheep and cattle. The meat was roasted (grilled over charcoal fires), boiled in broth, and dipped into highly seasoned sauces, as in the famous Mongolian Fire Pot dish. But the Chinese do not eat beef often. At one time, Buddhist vegetarianism discouraged it. Few cattle are raised, except for farm work, since land has never been spared for grazing. Beef dishes are not particularly popular in China. Pork and chicken are preferred.

Many beef dishes are simple stir fry with a vegetable or two, flavored with tasty seasonings such as oyster sauce, dried shellfish, or curry. Oyster sauce, a mixture of soy sauce and the broth from prolonged simmering of oysters, has a delicate, distinctive taste. Cantonese stir-fried beef dishes, like Oyster Sauce Beef and Steak with Pea Pods, are popular because the flavor of the quickly seared beef is sealed in and the vegetables stay crisp. Our recipes for stir-fried beef produce the same results as the conventional method.

Curry spices and slow-cooked Indian food were introduced through trade with southern Asia and are fairly popular in Canton. Our recipe for Curry Beef is a typical dish with onions and browned beef simmered in a curry sauce.

Tofu (bean curd), a product of soy beans, complements beef well, absorbing flavors and providing a contrast in texture. In our Spicy Beef with Tofu, the bland bean curd balances the rich, spicy zest of fermented black beans and chili peppers.

牛肉炒乾蠔

BEEF WITH DRIED OYSTERS

Servings: 4 to 6   Cooking time: 7½ minutes

10 dried oysters
1 tablespoon plus 1 teaspoon dry sherry
2 tablespoons plus 1 teaspoon soy sauce
2 tablespoons reserved oyster broth
1 large green pepper, cut in ⅛-inch strips
½ teaspoon vegetable oil
1 pound beef sirloin
1 teaspoon cornstarch
¼ teaspoon salt

Place dried oysters in small heatproof bowl or cup. Add water to cover. Heat on High 2 minutes. Let stand 10 minutes inside or outside oven. Drain oysters and clean well, reserving 2 table-spoons broth. Slice oysters in thin strips.

Place oysters in small heatproof cup. Add 1 teaspoon dry sherry, 1 teaspoon soy sauce, and 2 tablespoons broth. Cook on High 1 minute. Reserve.

Add oil to pepper slices. Place in heatproof dish, and cook on High ½ minute. Reserve.

Slice beef in strips ⅛ inch thick by 2 inches long. Add and mix the following, one at a time: the remaining sherry, the remaining soy sauce, 2 tablespoons cornstarch, and salt.

Combine meat and oyster mixture, arrange in heatproof dish, leaving center open. Cook on High 2 minutes. Stir, leave center open, and cook on High 1 minute more. Add partially cooked peppers, mix, leave center open, and cook on High 1 minute more.

清炒牛肉絲
BEEF WITH SCALLIONS

Servings: 4 to 6   Cooking time: 4½ minutes

1 pound top round steak
3 tablespoons soy sauce
1 tablespoon plus 1 teaspoon vegetable oil
2 teaspoons dry sherry
½ teaspoon sugar
2 scallions, sliced ⅛ inch thick
3 to 6 slices ginger root, shredded

Slice beef in strips ⅛ inch by 2 inches long and put in bowl. Combine soy sauce, 1 tablespoon oil, sherry, and sugar and pour over beef.

Mix together scallions, ginger slices, and remaining 1 teaspoon oil. Arrange evenly in large heatproof dish. Cook on High ½ minute.

Add beef to scallion mixture. Arrange in even layer, leaving center open. Cook on High 1 minute. Stir. Rearrange mixture, leaving center open. Cook on High 1½ minutes. Stir. Cook on High 1½ minutes more. Stir.

TIPS

Meat can be easily and evenly sliced when partially frozen.

Cooking time for meat results in medium rare beef. For more doneness, cook 1 minute at a time and test.

Stir-fried Broccoli is an excellent choice of vegetable for this dish.

咖哩牛肉
CURRY BEEF

Servings: 4 to 6   Cooking time: 19 minutes

½ cup flour
1 pound stew beef, cut in 1-inch cubes
1 medium size yellow onion, sliced in ¼-inch-thick rings
2 teaspoons vegetable oil
2 tablespoons dry sherry
2 tablespoons soy sauce
2 teaspoons curry powder (Malaysian curry preferred)
½ teaspoon salt
½ cup water

Place flour in bag and add beef cubes a few at a time. Shake to coat beef lightly. Remove and reserve beef.

Sprinkle onion rings with 1 teaspoon oil. Arrange onions in heatproof dish, leaving center open. Cook on High 1 minute. Reserve. (Onions are partially cooked.)

Add remaining teaspoon oil to browning dish. Preheat on High 5 minutes. Place coated meat on one half of heated dish. Cook on High 1 minute. Turn meat over onto unused half of dish. Cook on High 2 minutes.

Combine remaining ingredients and pour over meat. Mix well. Mix in reserved onions. Cover dish, and cook on High 2 minutes. Give dish a quarter turn. Cook on High 3 minutes. Give dish a quarter turn. Cook on High 5 minutes.

雪豆牛肉

FLANK STEAK AND PEA PODS

Servings: 4 to 6   Cooking time: 5 minutes

1 pound flank steak
3 tablespoons soy sauce
2 teaspoons dry sherry
1 teaspoon cornstarch
1 tablespoon plus 1 teaspoon vegetable oil
1 cup snow peas (pea pods)
1 thin slice ginger, slivered

Slice steak in strips ¼ inch thick by 2 inches long, and put into bowl. Stir in the following, one at a time: soy sauce, sherry, cornstarch, 1 tablespoon oil, ginger slivers. Marinate steak 10 minutes at room temperature. The marinade will be absorbed by the meat.

Sprinkle remaining oil over snow peas and stir. Arrange in heatproof dish in even layer, leaving center open. Cook on High 1 minute. Reserve.

Arrange marinated steak in even layer in heatproof dish, leaving center open. Cook on High 2 minutes. Stir. Give dish a quarter turn. Cook on High 2 minutes more. Stir in reserved snow peas. Let stand 2 minutes.

TIPS
Meat can be sliced easily and evenly when partially frozen.

Cooking time results in medium rare beef. For more doneness cook 1 minute at a time and test.

生菜包
LETTUCE ROLLS

Servings: 4 to 6   Cooking time: 5 minutes

½ pound ground beef
½ teaspoon salt
1½ teaspoons sugar
½ teaspoon cornstarch
1 teaspoon plus a few drops sesame oil (optional)
2 teaspoons soy sauce
2 tablespoons water
Dash black pepper
½ cup diced green peppers
½ cup diced bamboo shoots
½ cup diced carrots
2 scallions, chopped
1 tablespoon hoisin sauce
Iceberg lettuce leaves, whole

Arrange beef in thin layer in heatproof dish, leaving center open. Cook on High 1 minute. Stir well, breaking up any clumps of meat. Leaving center open, cook on High 1 minute more. Stir well. Drain off and discard any liquid.

Add to meat and mix well: salt, ½ teaspoon sugar, cornstarch, 1 teaspoon sesame oil (if used), soy sauce, water, and black pepper. Stir in peppers, bamboo shoots, carrots, and all but 2 teaspoons of the chopped scallions. Cook on High 3 minutes. Stir. Let stand 1 minute.

In small bowl combine hoisin sauce, remaining 1 teaspoon sugar, the remaining 2 teaspoons scallions, and a few drops sesame oil (if used). Brush one side of each lettuce leaf generously with this mixture.

On moistened side of leaf and near bottom, place about 2 tablespoons beef mixture. Starting at bottom of leaf, roll lettuce over stuffing, folding in sides in envelope fashion. Finish rolling up leaf. Repeat with lettuce leaves until all stuffing has been used.

Serve to be eaten sandwich style.

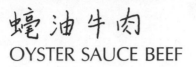

OYSTER SAUCE BEEF

Servings: 4 to 6   Cooking time: 3 minutes

1 pound beef sirloin
1 thin slice ginger root, minced
1 tablespoon dry sherry
5 tablespoons oyster sauce
1 teaspoon cornstarch
1 scallion, slivered, for garnish
1 carrot, slivered, for garnish

Slice beef in strips ⅛ inch thick by 2 inches long. Sprinkle ginger over beef slices. Add the following one at a time, mixing well after each addition: sherry, oyster sauce, cornstarch. Arrange beef slices evenly in large heatproof dish. Cook on High 2 minutes. Stir. Give dish a quarter turn. Cook on High 1 minute more. Garnish while hot.

TIPS
Meat can be sliced easily and evenly when partially frozen.

Cooking time results in medium rare beef. For more doneness, cook 1 minute at a time and test.

Stir-fried vegetables are excellent side dishes to serve with this dish. Cook vegetables as directed in Chapter 8.

辣子豆腐
SZECHUAN SPICY BEEF WITH TOFU

Servings: 4 to 6   Cooking time: 9½ minutes

2 teaspoons fermented, salted black beans
Sauce (see below)
5 to 6 dried Chinese mushrooms
1 cake tofu (bean curd), about 1 pound drained
1 pound ground beef

4 garlic cloves, minced
3 scallions, thinly sliced

Place beans and ½ cup water in 1-cup heatproof measure. Heat on High ½ minute. Let stand 5 minutes, in or out of oven. Drain and add beans to sauce.

Rinse mushrooms, and place in 1-quart heatproof measure with 1 cup warm water. Cover with plastic wrap, leaving small vent. Heat on High 4 minutes. Let stand 5 minutes, in or out of oven. Remove hard stems and discard. Cut mushrooms in quarters and reserve.

Rinse tofu in water, drain. Cut in ½-inch cubes. Reserve.

Arrange beef in heatproof dish in even layer, leaving center open. Cook on High 2 minutes. Drain off juices and discard. Add mushrooms, garlic, and scallions, and mix lightly with a fork. Add sauce and stir lightly.

Drain any additional liquid from diced bean curd. Add bean curd to meat mixture. Stir gently.

Rearrange mixture evenly in large heatproof dish, leaving center open. Cook on High 3 minutes. Let stand about 5 minutes, in or out of oven, to blend flavors.

SAUCE
2 tablespoons soy sauce
2 tablespoons hoisin sauce
2 teaspoons American chili sauce or ketchup
1 teaspoon sugar
4 tablespoons chicken broth, homemade or canned
1 to 2 teaspoons Szechuan-style chili sauce, or ½ to 1 teaspoon
    crushed red pepper
1 teaspoon sesame oil

Mix ingredients together.

TIP
See page 119 for a recipe for homemade Szechuan-style Chili Sauce.

青椒牛肉絲
STIR-FRIED BEEF WITH PEPPERS

Servings: 4 to 6   Cooking time: 9½ minutes

1 pound flank steak
3 tablespoons soy sauce
2 tablespoons dry sherry
1 teaspoon cornstarch
¼ teaspoon sugar
2 tablespoons plus 1 teaspoon vegetable oil
¼ teaspoon salt
1 medium size yellow onion, cut in ⅛-inch slices
1 green pepper, cut in ⅛-inch slices
3 to 5 thin slices ginger root
1 scallion, slivered, for garnish

Slice steak in strips ⅛ inch thick by 2 inches long and put in bowl. Combine soy sauce, sherry, cornstarch, and sugar, and pour over meat. Marinate 10 minutes.

Mix 1 teaspoon oil and salt with onion and green pepper slices. Arrange vegetables on large heatproof dish. Cook on High 1 minute. Remove from dish and reserve.

To same dish add remaining 2 tablespoons oil and ginger. Cook on High 5 minutes. Remove ginger and discard. Stir in marinated meat slices. Arrange evenly, leaving center open. Cook on High 2 minutes. Stir. Arrange evenly, leaving center open. Cook on High 1 minute more.

Stir in reserved onion and pepper slices. Arrange evenly. Cook on High ½ minute. Sprinkle slivered scallions over meat while hot.

TIPS
Meat can be easily and evenly sliced when partially frozen.

Cooking time for meat results in medium rare beef. For more doneness, cook 1 minute at a time and test. Then add vegetables and cook ½ minute longer.

4 · PORK

Pork is the most popular meat with the Chinese, who have created hundreds of dishes using every part of the pig from gizzard to skin. Their unsmoked, aged ham has no counterpart in this country, although the best substitute is Smithfield or Westphalian ham.

Increased trade with the Middle East and southern Asia and improved agriculture at home contributed to a growing repertoire of pork dishes using spices, grains, fruits, vegetables, and nuts. Our recipe for Red-cooked Pork and Chestnuts is a simple yet robust dish of quartered nuts and pork cubes, which complement each other in texture and size. Chestnuts from the northern province of Hopei are considered the finest although they are harvested in many other areas.

In a contrasting style, our Szechuan Pork recipe combines thin strips of pork and Chinese mushrooms with hot chili sauce for a lightly spiced dish typical of the region. Ground pork is used frequently in sauces, stuffings, and steamed and stir-fried dishes. Lion's Head Dumplings are very large dumplings of ground pork steamed on a bed of cabbage leaves. The dish gets its name from the supposed resemblance of the dumplings to the heads and the cabbage leaves to the manes of lions.

Just as Americans traditionally celebrate Thanksgiving with turkey, the Chinese prepare special dishes for holidays and religious observances. For the lunar New Year, large quantities of pork-and-cabbage-stuffed dumplings, Chiao Tze, are made ahead of time and may be kept frozen out-of-doors. Visiting relatives and friends are welcomed through the day with freshly cooked dumplings. We have a recipe for this dish in Chapter 1.

Food sacrifices to ancestral spirits were common in the folk religion rituals of southern China. The highest level offering of the Cantonese was a roasted whole pig for which they sought the blessings of health, happiness, and wealth.

獅子頭
LION'S HEAD DUMPLINGS

Servings: 4 to 6   Cooking time: 14 minutes

½ pound celery cabbage
1 teaspoon vegetable oil
¼ teaspoon salt
1 pound coarsely ground pork (preferably shoulder)
4 to 6 thin slices ginger root, finely chopped
2 to 3 scallions, chopped
1 tablespoon dry sherry
2 tablespoons plus 1 teaspoon soy sauce
2 teaspoons sesame oil
1 egg, unbeaten
½ pound tofu (bean curd), drained, cut into ½-inch cubes

Cut cabbage lengthwise into 4 sections, then slice crosswise into 1½-inch sections. Add oil and salt. Mix well. Arrange cabbage in heatproof dish, leaving center open. Cover tightly. Cook on High 3 minutes. Uncover and reserve cabbage.

Combine pork, ginger, scallions, sherry, soy sauce, sesame oil, and mix well. Add egg and mix. Gently mix in tofu. Divide mixture into 8 portions. Form 8 large balls.

Arrange dumplings evenly spaced on partially cooked cabbage, leaving center open. Cover tightly. Cook on High 5 minutes. Give dish a quarter turn. Cook on High 6 minutes more.

TIP
An 8-by-8-inch square dish is a convenient size for this dish.

醬爆肉

PORK WITH HOISIN SAUCE

Servings: 4 to 6   Cooking time: 4½ minutes

½ pound pork shoulder
2 tablespoons soy sauce
1½ tablespoons ketchup
1½ tablespoons hoisin sauce
1 teaspoon dry sherry
1 teaspoon sugar
1 teaspoon American chili sauce
½ teaspoon vegetable oil
1½ teaspoons cornstarch mixed with 3 tablespoons water
½ pound fresh mushrooms, cut in ¼-inch-thick slices

Slice pork in pieces ⅛ inch thick by 2 inches long.

Mix together soy sauce, ketchup, hoisin sauce, sherry, sugar, chili sauce, and oil. Marinate beef in one half of marinade 30 minutes. To remainder of marinade, add cornstarch mixture, and pour over marinated pork. Mix well. Arrange pork in heatproof dish in single layer, leaving center open. Cook on High 3 minutes. Stir in sliced mushrooms. Cook on High 1½ minutes more.

TIP
Stir-fried vegetables are excellent side dishes to serve with this dish. Cook vegetables as directed in Chapter 8.

栗子烧肉
RED-COOKED PORK WITH CHESTNUTS

Servings: 4 to 6   Cooking time: 25 minutes

2 cups raw European chestnuts (see Tip)
1 pound boneless pork (preferably shoulder)
2 slices ginger root
¼ cup soy sauce
2½ tablespoons dry sherry
1 teaspoon brown sugar
¼ teaspoon salt
½ cup broth

With a small sharp knife, cut an × in flat side of each chestnut and put them in a 2-quart heatproof bowl with 2 cups water. Cover with plastic wrap, leaving a small vent. Cook on High 5 minutes, give bowl a quarter turn and cook on High 6 minutes more. Let stand 5 minutes, inside or outside oven. Peel chestnuts, remove thin brown inner skin, cut in quarters, and reserve.

Cut pork into ½-inch cubes. Put cubes and ginger slices in 1-quart heatproof bowl with warm water to cover. Cover bowl with plastic wrap, leaving small vent. Cook on High until water boils, about 7 minutes. Drain, reserving ½ cup broth.

To pork, add soy sauce, sherry, brown sugar, salt, and reserved liquid. Mix well and stir in chestnuts.

Transfer mixture to shallow dish, spreading in an even layer, leaving center open. Cover tightly with plastic wrap, and cook on High 7 minutes.

TIPS
Cutting an × in chestnuts makes shelling easier. Brown inner skin should be removed because of slight bitter taste.

Dried chestnuts may be used in place of fresh chestnuts. Put 1 cup dried chestnuts and 2 cups water in heatproof 4-cup measure. Cover, leaving a vent, and place in oven away from center. Heat on High 7 minutes. Let stand 10 minutes. Drain off water. Remove any pieces of brown inner skin.

Ginger slices may be discarded after pork is cooked, or left in dish if preferred.

芝蔴香肉
SESAME PORK TENDERLOIN

Servings: 4 to 6   Cooking time: 13 minutes

¼ cup sesame seeds, toasted
1- to 1½-pound whole pork tenderloin
⅔ cup water
½ cup soy sauce
4 tablespoons chopped scallions
1 tablespoon vegetable oil
2 garlic cloves, minced
2 teaspoons minced ginger root

Spread sesame seeds in thin layer in heatproof dish, leaving center open. Toast on High 5 minutes. Stir. Crush seeds somewhat. Reserve.

Place tenderloin in dish. Combine water, soy sauce, scallions, oil, garlic, and ginger and pour over meat. Sprinkle sesame seeds over pork. Cover, leaving small vent. Cook on High 5 minutes. Give dish a quarter turn. Baste pork with sauce. Re-cover, leaving small vent. Cook on High 3 minutes more. Serve.

TIP

If pork shows any pink, continue cooking 1 minute at a time and test. Avoid overcooking. Tenderloin cooks more rapidly than other cuts of pork.

甜燒排骨
SOY SAUCE SPARERIBS

Servings: 4 to 6   Cooking time: 20 minutes

2 pounds small pork spareribs, cut in 1-inch pieces
1 tablespoon vegetable oil
½ cup reserved broth
½ cup scallions, cut in 1-inch pieces
¼ cup soy sauce
2 tablespoons sugar
1 tablespoon dark soy sauce
1 tablespoon dry sherry
1 teaspoon hoisin sauce
1 teaspoon cornstarch
2 thin slices ginger root, shredded

Sprinkle sparerib pieces with oil. Spread in single layer in large heatproof dish. Cover, leaving small vent. Cook on High 5 minutes. Give dish a quarter turn. Cook on High 5 minutes more. Let stand 5 minutes.

Drain off juices and reserve ½ cup broth. Combine the reserved broth with the remaining ingredients and pour over ribs. Cover, leaving small vent. Cook on High 5 minutes.

TIP
Have spareribs cut in pieces when purchased, or cut into individual ribs and chop into pieces with cleaver or knife.

肉絲白菜

STIR-FRIED PORK WITH BOK CHOY

Servings: 4 to 6   Cooking time: 11 minutes

½ pound pork shoulder
1 tablespoon plus 2 teaspoons soy sauce
1 tablespoon dry sherry
2 teaspoons cornstarch
½ teaspoon salt
1 tablespoon vegetable oil
1 pound bok choy, cut at an angle crosswise into ¼-inch slices

Slice pork in pieces ¼ inch thick by 2 inches long. Combine soy sauce, sherry, cornstarch, and ¼ teaspoon salt. Add pork, mix well, and marinate 10 minutes.

Add oil to bok choy slices and mix. Place in even layer in large heatproof dish, leaving center open. Cook on High 1 minute. Sprinkle with remaining salt and mix. Reserve.

Arrange pork in even layer in heatproof dish, leaving center open. Cover, leaving small vent. Cook on High 3 minutes. Give dish a quarter turn. Cook on High 3 minutes more. Uncover and mix in bok choy and cook on High 2 minutes. Stir. Give dish a quarter turn. Cook on High 2 minutes more.

TIP

Other vegetables can be substituted for bok choy. If celery cabbage is used, cook for 5 minutes. Cook snow peas 3 minutes, or bean sprouts 2 minutes. Then follow rest of procedure.

黄瓜釀肉
STUFFED CUCUMBERS WITH PORK

Servings: 4 to 6   Cooking time: 10 minutes

½ pound ground pork
2 tablespoons soy sauce
2 tablespoons chopped scallions
1 tablespoon minced ginger root
1 teaspoon dry sherry
½ teaspoon salt
1 egg, lightly beaten
4 medium size cucumbers, peeled
4 tablespoons chicken broth, homemade or canned

Combine pork, soy sauce, 1 tablespoon scallions, ginger, sherry, salt, and egg. Mix well.

Cut off small pieces from ends of cucumbers. Slice each cucumber crosswise into 4 pieces, about 1½ inches long. Remove seeds and discard. Fill centers of pieces with pork mixture.

Arrange stuffed cucumbers on end in heatproof dish in single layer, leaving center open. Sprinkle chicken broth over cucumbers. Then scatter remaining 1 tablespoon scallions over all. Cover tightly. Cook on High 5 minutes. Give dish a quarter turn. Cook on High 5 minutes more. Let stand, in or out of oven, covered, 3 to 4 minutes. Serve hot.

四川辣肉

SZECHUAN PORK

Servings: 4 to 6   Cooking time: 11 minutes

1 pound pork tenderloin
4 to 5 dried Chinese mushrooms
3 tablespoons soy sauce
2 tablespoons dry sherry
2 tablespoons vegetable oil
1 tablespoon cornstarch
2 to 3 slices ginger root, chopped
½ to 1 teaspoon Szechuan-style chili sauce, or more to taste

Slice pork into strips, ⅛ inch thick by 2 inches long.

Rinse mushrooms and place in 1-quart heatproof measure with 1 cup warm water. Cover with plastic wrap, leaving small vent. Heat on High 4 minutes. Let stand 5 minutes, in or out of oven. Remove hard stems and discard. Cut in ⅛-inch strips and reserve.

Combine soy sauce, sherry, oil, cornstarch, and ginger. Mix, and marinate pork slices and mushrooms in this mixture 15 minutes. Arrange evenly in heatproof dish, leaving center open. Cover and cook on High 4 minutes. Add chili sauce and stir well. Spread meat evenly in dish, leaving center open. Re-cover and cook on High 3 minutes more.

TIPS
Meat can be easily and evenly sliced when partially frozen.

Recipe for homemade Szechuan-style Chili Sauce is on page 119.

Always rinse dried mushrooms before soaking to remove small particles that can cause too much foaming when they are heated in water and result in overflow from the bowl.

鴰 鴨

5 · POULTRY

Kitchen murals and records in ancient Han tombs show that fowl was prepared in many ways, by shallow and deep frying, roasting, and stewing. Red-cooking, a speciality of southern China, is a way of simmering meat until very tender in a large quantity of soy sauce flavored with star anise. The skin acquires a rich reddish brown color. We have included recipes for red-cooked chicken and duck in this chapter. The soy sauce mixture can be reused several times, occasionally replenished with seasonings, much like a French stock pot. By contrast, White Cut Chicken is a Cantonese dish. The chicken is simmered in its own juices and mild seasonings with nothing added to change the natural color and flavor. It is always carved in small pieces and served cold with a dip. We have included illustrations showing how to carve fowl and the traditional rearrangement of the pieces.

Centuries ago, sesame seeds were imported from the Middle East and quickly assimilated into Chinese cooking. The oil is valued as a seasoning and the seeds for cakes and candies. In the chicken salad recipe in this chapter, sesame seeds add a contrast in texture and taste.

栗子雞丁
CHICKEN WITH CHESTNUTS

Servings: 4 to 6   Cooking time: 23 minutes

2 cups raw European chestnuts (see Tip)
2 cups warm water
1 tablespoon vegetable oil
2 slices ginger root, cut in strips
1 pound chicken, skin removed, cut in ½-inch cubes
½ cup chicken broth, homemade or canned
1 tablespoon soy sauce
1 tablespoon dry sherry
½ teaspoon salt

With small sharp knife, cut an × in flat side of each chestnut and put them in a 2-quart heatproof bowl with water. Cover with plastic wrap, leaving small vent. Cook on High 5 minutes. Give bowl a quarter turn. Cook on High 6 minutes more. Let stand 5 minutes, inside or outside oven. Peel chestnuts, removing thin brown skin. Cut in quarters and reserve.

To large shallow heatproof dish add oil and ginger strips. Cook on High 1 minute, remove ginger. Heat oil, uncovered, on High 2 minutes. Add chicken and stir. Arrange, leaving center open. Cook on High 2 minutes. Stir. Rearrange, leaving center open. Cook on High 1 minute. Combine broth, soy sauce, sherry, and salt and add to chicken mixture. Mix well. Add reserved chestnuts and mix. Arrange in even layer, leaving center open. Cover with plastic wrap. Cook on High 4 minutes. Give dish a quarter turn. Cook on High 2 minutes more.

TIPS
Cutting an × in each chestnut shell makes removal of shell easier after cooking. Removal of thin inner skins is preferred because of slight bitter taste.

Dried chestnuts may be used in place of fresh chestnuts. Put 1 cup dried chestnuts and 2 cups water in heatproof 4-cup measure. Cover, leaving vent, and place in oven away from center. Heat on

High 7 minutes. Let stand 10 minutes. Drain off water. Remove any pieces of brown inner skin.

Canned chicken broth tends to be salty.

涼熱拌雞塊

COLD OR HOT CHICKEN SALAD

Servings: 4 to 6   Cooking time: 6 minutes

1 pound raw chicken breasts, boned and skinned
1 tablespoon vegetable oil
¼ teaspoon hot red pepper (cayenne), or more to taste
3 to 4 thin slices ginger root, minced
1 tablespoon soy sauce
1 tablespoon vinegar
1½ teaspoons sugar
½ teaspoon salt
½ teaspoon sesame oil (optional)
1 scallion, chopped
2 tablespoons sesame seeds

Place chicken breasts in heatproof dish in single layer. Cover. Cook on High 2 minutes. Turn breasts over. Re-cover tightly. Cook on High 1½ minutes. Cool slightly.

Cut chicken into ½-inch cubes. Reserve.

To a small, deep, heatproof dish or cup add oil, red pepper, and ginger. Mix. Heat on High 2½ minutes or until oil is hot. Combine soy sauce, vinegar, sugar, salt, and sesame oil and add to hot oil. Mix. Add scallion and stir. Pour sauce mixture over chicken cubes. Toss lightly. Sprinkle chicken with sesame seeds. Toss lightly. Serve hot or cold.

TIP
When prepared ahead and refrigerated, chicken salad is an excellent hot weather dish that can be served with a vegetable from Chapter 8.

烧滷雞
BARBECUE CHICKEN

Servings: 4 to 6   Cooking time: 20 minutes

½ cup soy sauce
¼ cup dry sherry
1 tablespoon brown sugar
1 teaspoon salt, or more to taste
2 pounds cut up chicken
1 large yellow onion, cut in 1-inch pieces
1 green bell pepper, cut in 1-inch squares

Combine soy sauce, sherry, brown sugar, salt, green pepper, and onions, and marinate chicken in mixture 10 minutes. Drain off marinade and discard. Arrange chicken in heatproof dish, leaving center open. Cover with plastic wrap, leaving small vent. Cook on High 10 minutes. Give dish a quarter turn. Cook on High 10 minutes more.

黃瓜拌雞片
SZECHUAN CHICKEN WITH CUCUMBERS

Servings: 4 to 6   Cooking time: 3½ minutes

1 pound raw chicken breasts, boned and skinned
2 cucumbers, peeled, cut in ¼-inch strips
1 teaspoon salt, or to taste
1 tablespoon soy sauce
¼ cup sesame oil
¼ teaspoon Chinese hot pepper oil, or to taste

Place chicken in shallow heatproof dish. Cover tightly with plastic wrap. Cook on High 2 minutes. Give dish a quarter turn. Turn breasts over. Re-cover tightly. Cook on High 1½ minutes more.

Cut chicken across grain into ¼-inch slices. Mix chicken with cucumbers, salt, soy sauce, sesame oil, and hot pepper oil. Toss well. Serve hot or chilled.

TIP
When salad is served cold, 1 tablespoon vinegar and ¼ teaspoon sugar may be added.

冬菇蒸雞片
STEAMED CHICKEN WITH CHINESE MUSHROOMS

Servings: 4 to 6   Cooking time: 7 minutes

8 to 10 dried Chinese mushrooms, whole
1 pound raw chicken, boned and skinned
2 tablespoons dry sherry
1 tablespoon soy sauce
½ teaspoon sugar
½ teaspoon salt
1 teaspoon vegetable oil
2 to 3 slices ginger root, cut in thin strips

Rinse mushrooms, and place in 1-quart heatproof measure with 1 cup warm water. Cover with plastic wrap, leaving small vent. Heat on High 4 minutes. Let stand 5 minutes, inside or outside oven. Remove hard stems and discard. Reserve.

Cut chicken across grain in ¼-inch slices. Sprinkle sherry, soy sauce, sugar, salt, oil, and ginger strips over chicken. Stir and mix well. Arrange chicken evenly in heatproof dish, leaving center open. Cover with plastic wrap, leaving small vent. Cook on High 2 minutes. Stir. Arrange mushrooms over chicken, leaving center open. Re-cover, leaving small vent. Cook on High 1 minute more. If chicken needs more cooking, let stand for 2 or 3 minutes, inside or outside oven.

TIP
Always rinse dried mushrooms before soaking to remove small particles that can cause too much foaming when they are heated in water and result in overflow from the bowl.

咖 喱 雞
CURRY CHICKEN

Servings: 4 to 6   Cooking time: 3½ minutes

1 pound raw chicken breasts, boned and skinned
1 tablespoon dry sherry
1 tablespoon cornstarch
1 egg, slightly beaten
2 teaspoons curry powder (Malaysian curry preferred)
½ teaspoon salt
1 tablespoon vegetable oil
Cilantro (Chinese parsley) for garnish (optional)

Cut chicken across grain into ¼-inch slices. Add, one at a time, and mix well: sherry, cornstarch, egg, curry powder, salt, and oil.

Arrange chicken in heatproof dish in even layer, leaving center open. Cook on High 2 minutes. Stir.

Rearrange chicken in even layer, leaving center open. Cook on High 1½ minutes more. Stir. If chicken requires slightly more cooking, let stand a few minutes. Garnish, if desired, with cilantro.

TIP
Shimmery Bok Choy (see page 96) is an excellent vegetable to serve with Curry Chicken.

紅燒雞
RED-COOKED CHICKEN

Servings: 4 to 6   Cooking time: 25 minutes

8 scallions, cut in 1½-inch lengths
¾ cup soy sauce
¼ cup dry sherry
2 tablespoons brown sugar, packed
2 teaspoons minced ginger root
½ teaspoon five-spice powder
1 garlic clove, minced
1 2½-pound chicken, cut into 8 to 10 pieces
2 tablespoons slivered scallions

Combine scallions, soy sauce, sherry, sugar, ginger, five-spice powder, and garlic, and mix well. Dip each chicken piece into this sauce. Arrange in single layer in large heatproof dish and pour sauce over. Cover tightly with plastic wrap. Cook on High 13 minutes. Give dish a quarter turn. Baste chicken with sauce. Re-cover tightly and cook on High 12 minutes more. While hot, sprinkle with slivered scallions.

TIPS
Dry chicken pieces thoroughly before dipping into sauce to assure good absorption.

    After the fowl has been cooked in the soy sauce mixture, the volume increases due to the juices from the fowl. Drain off the sauce and refrigerate. It keeps in the refrigerator for 1 to 2 weeks and may be reused several times. If frozen, it keeps for many months.

白切雞

WHITE CUT CHICKEN

Servings: 4 to 6   Cooking time: 12 minutes

1 2- to 3-pound chicken, whole
2 slices ginger root, cut in thin strips
1 large or 2 small scallions, cut in 2-inch pieces
½ cup water
Dip sauce (see below)

Wash chicken. Put 1 piece of scallion and half the ginger strips into chicken cavity. Put chicken, breast up, in deep heatproof bowl, and sprinkle rest of ginger and scallions on top. Add water to bowl and cover tightly with plastic wrap.

Cook on High 8 minutes. Turn chicken over, re-cover tightly, and cook on High 3 minutes more. Test near bone for doneness. Chicken should be plump and juicy. If more cooking is needed, re-cover and cook on High 1 minute at a time, and test for doneness. Do not overcook.

Cool chicken to room temperature and refrigerate. Before serving, cut into small pieces as shown. Carved chicken may be arranged in the shape of whole chicken for attractive appearance. Serve with hot or cold dip sauce.

DIP SAUCE
2 slices ginger, minced
1 scallion, chopped
3 tablespoons soy sauce
½ teaspoon vegetable oil
¼ teaspoon dry sherry
¼ teaspoon sugar

Mix all ingredients together in small heatproof bowl or 1-cup measure, and cook on High 1 minute. Dip can be served hot or cold.

TIPS
White Cut Chicken can be served as an appetizer.

Chicken and dip sauce can be prepared ahead of time and refrigerated until served.

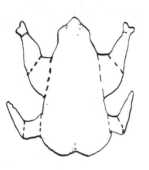

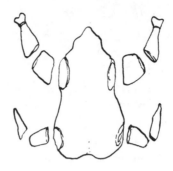

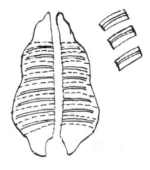

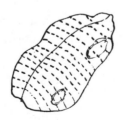

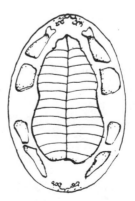

SOY SAUCE CHICKEN

Servings: 4 to 6   Cooking time: 24 minutes

1 3- to 3½-pound chicken, whole
¾ cup soy sauce
¼ cup dark soy sauce
5 tablespoons sugar
1 teaspoon dry sherry
1 teaspoon sesame oil
1 teaspoon salt
1 slice ginger root, ¼ inch thick
1 scallion, cut in 3-inch sections

Place chicken in a heatproof bowl that is just large enough to hold fowl and sauce.

Combine soy sauces, sugar, sherry, sesame oil, and salt. Pour over chicken and turn to coat evenly. Turn breast down with ginger and scallion on top. Cover tightly. Cook on High 12 minutes. Turn chicken breast up and give dish a quarter turn. Re-cover and cook on High 12 to 16 minutes, depending on weight. Cut chicken into serving pieces following carving instructions illustrated on page 67.

TIPS

Dark soy sauce is heavier than regular soy sauce and it makes skin darker.

Dry chicken thoroughly to insure good absorption of sauce.

After the fowl has been cooked in the soy sauce mixture, the volume increases due to the juices from the fowl. Drain off the sauce and refrigerate. It keeps in the refrigerator for 1 to 2 weeks and may be reused several times. If frozen, it keeps for many months.

紅 燒 鴨
RED-COOKED DUCK

Servings: 4 to 6   Cooking time: 42 minutes

1 4- to 4½-pound duck, whole
¾ cup soy sauce
¼ cup dry sherry
2 tablespoons brown sugar, packed
1 tablespoon dark soy sauce
2 teaspoons minced ginger root
½ teaspoon five-spice powder
8 scallions, cut in 1½-inch lengths
1 garlic clove, minced

Remove internal fat deposits from duck. Cut off fatty tissue around neck and central cavity and discard. Dry duck thoroughly, inside and out.

Place duck on one side in heatproof bowl with wing and leg on bottom. Cover tightly with plastic wrap and cook on High 6 minutes. Turn duck over with opposite wing and leg on bottom. Re-cover and cook on High 6 minutes more. Drain off fat. Turn duck breast up. Re-cover and cook on High 5 minutes. Give bowl a quarter turn. Cook on High 5 minutes more. Drain off fat.

Combine remaining ingredients and pour over duck. Turn breast down. Cover and cook on High 10 minutes. Baste. Turn breast up and re-cover. Cook on High 10 minutes more. Baste. Cut duck into serving pieces as shown on page 67.

TIPS
Addition of dark soy sauce contributes to rich dark color of skin.

After the fowl has been cooked in the soy sauce mixture, the volume increases due to the juices from the fowl. Drain off the sauce and refrigerate. It keeps refrigerated for 1 to 2 weeks and may be reused; frozen, it keeps many months.

Traditionally, some fat remains between the skin and flesh of the duck. Turning the duck and draining the liquefied fat as described removes a great deal of fat, leaving a thin layer of firm, flavorful fat between the chewy skin and tender meat.

海鮮

6 · SEAFOOD

In the thirteenth century, Marco Polo marveled at the busy Hangchow boat traffic bringing fresh sea cucumbers, jellyfish, squid, mullet, grouper, and shellfish from the China Sea, giant sturgeon from the great rivers, and freshwater eel and carp. Long ago, the Chinese developed the first pond carp farms. Even today they prefer to buy carp live, and freshwater holding tanks are a common sight in their markets.

Chinese cooks are careful to choose the right fish and sauce for a seafood dish. Texture, taste, and color are important. Our recipe for the classic Steamed Fish in Black Bean Sauce calls for a firm-fleshed, flavorsome fish like scrod, haddock, bass, or whitefish sturdy enough for marinating and steaming. Flounder and sole are too delicate for this dish. The piquant, salty black beans mellow during cooking and blend with the fish juices into a rich dark sauce. The short cooking times should be followed carefully since a whole fish will cook in a few minutes.

Our microwave stir-fried recipes produce unusually succulent shellfish. Many distinctive dishes can be prepared with our basic recipes by varying the vegetables and sauces. You should select a sauce that enhances the flavor, delicately seasoned for scallops, but light or spicy for shrimps, clams, and oysters.

In China, a fish course signaled the finale of an elaborate banquet. Since the word for fish also means abundance, guests were served a dish so large and lavish that no one could leave hungry.

70

冬菇烧魚片
FISH FILETS WITH CHINESE MUSHROOMS

Servings: 4 to 6   Cooking time: 9 minutes

2 dried Chinese mushrooms
1¼ pounds fresh filets, cod or haddock
2 tablespoons dry sherry
1 tablespoon plus 1 teaspoon soy sauce
2 teaspoons vegetable oil
¼ teaspoon salt
¼ teaspoon sugar
1 scallion, cut in thin strips
2 to 3 thin slices ginger root, cut in thin strips

Rinse mushrooms and place in 1-quart heatproof measure with 1 cup warm water. Cover with plastic wrap, leaving small vent. Heat on High 4 minutes. Let stand 5 minutes, in or out of oven. Remove hard stems and discard. Cut in ⅛-inch strips and reserve.

Pat fish filets dry. Combine sherry, soy sauce, oil, salt, and sugar and pour over fish, turning to cover. Marinate fish for 10 minutes at room temperature.

Place fish in one layer in heatproof dish large enough to hold all filets, leaving center open. Sprinkle mushrooms, scallion, and ginger over filets. Cook on High 5 minutes.

TIPS
For frozen fish, see thawing directions in the manufacturer's manual for your microwave oven.

Always rinse dried mushrooms before cooking to remove small particles that can cause too much foaming when they are heated in water and result in overflow from the bowl.

龍虾糊燴魚片

FISH IN LOBSTER SAUCE WITH BLACK BEANS

Servings: 4 to 6   Cooking time: 13 minutes

2 teaspoons fermented, salted black beans
1 clove garlic, minced
5 teaspoons vegetable oil
¼ pound ground pork
½ cup water
1 tablespoon soy sauce
1 tablespoon dry sherry
½ teaspoon sugar
2 scallions, cut in ½-inch pieces
1 tablespoon cornstarch
2 eggs, slightly beaten
1 pound haddock filets
½ teaspoon salt

Soak beans in warm water 10 minutes. Drain and chop coarsely. Mix beans with garlic to form a paste. Reserve.

Add 4 teaspoons oil to heatproof dish. Cover and heat on High 5 minutes. Add bean-garlic paste and pork. Stir and spread evenly. Cook on High 1 minute and reserve.

Mix together water, soy sauce, sherry, sugar, scallions, and cornstarch. Add to bean-pork mixture and mix well. Cover and cook on High 3 minutes. Add eggs and stir gently, allowing eggs to set. Reserve.

Place fish in one layer in heatproof dish, leaving center open. Brush fish with remaining 1 teaspoon oil and sprinkle with salt. Cook on High 3 minutes. Pour reserved mixture over fish and cook on High 1 minute more.

TIP

This sauce does not contain lobster. It is served on lobster, shrimp, and fish. It is also called fish sauce indicating that it may be used with a variety of shellfish and fish.

豆豉青蒸魚

STEAMED FISH IN BLACK BEAN SAUCE

Servings: 4 to 6   Cooking time: 6 minutes

1 teaspoon fermented, salted black beans, coarsely chopped
1 tablespoon dry sherry
1 tablespoon soy sauce
2 teaspoons vegetable oil
1½ pounds whole firm fish, any nonoily fish such as scrod, haddock,
   bass, or whitefish
1 teaspoon salt
1 scallion, cut in 4-inch-long strips
3 thin slices ginger root, cut in thin strips

Combine black beans, sherry, soy sauce, and oil. Rinse fish in cold water. Dry well, inside and out. Slit fish lengthwise into 2 pieces. Make two or three deep crosscuts in skin of each piece. Rub each fish piece on both sides with salt.

Place fish slices, skin side up, in large heatproof dish. Pour black bean sauce over fish. Sprinkle scallion and ginger strips over top of fish. Marinate fish for 15 to 20 minutes. Cover dish tightly with plastic wrap. Cook on High 6 minutes.

TIP
If additional cooking is needed because of greater weight or thickness of fish slices, cook uncovered on High 1 minute at a time and test for doneness. Avoid overcooking. Fish will be cooked when it loses its transparency and can be flaked with a fork.

糖醋全魚
SWEET-AND-SOUR FISH

Servings: 4 to 6   Cooking time: 14 minutes

¼ cup cider or white vinegar
6 tablespoons sugar
1½ tablespoons cornstarch mixed with ½ cup water
1 tablespoon ketchup
1 tablespoon soy sauce
2 teaspoons salt
4 to 5 dried Chinese mushrooms
1½ pound whole firm fish, such as scrod, haddock, bass, or whitefish
1 tablespoon vegetable oil
1 scallion, shredded
Cilantro (Chinese parsley) or Italian parsley for garnish (optional)

In small deep heatproof bowl, mix together vinegar, sugar, cornstarch mixture, ketchup, soy sauce, and 1 teaspoon salt. Cook on High 4 minutes and reserve.

Rinse mushrooms, and place in 1-quart heatproof measure with 1 cup warm water. Cover with plastic wrap, leaving small vent. Heat on High 4 minutes. Let stand 5 minutes, inside or outside oven. Remove hard stems and discard. Cut in ⅛-inch thin slices and add to reserved sauce.

Rub remaining salt over inside and outside of fish. Brush oil on outside of fish. Place flat in heatproof dish. Cover. Cook on High 3 minutes. Turn fish over. Re-cover dish and cook on High 3 minutes more. Pour reserved sauce over fish. Sprinkle shredded scallion over hot fish.

TIPS
For a larger fish, slightly longer cooking time will be needed. Cook, covered on High 1 minute at a time and test for doneness. Avoid overcooking.

Always rinse dried mushrooms before soaking to remove small particles that can cause too much foaming when they are heated in water and result in overflow from the bowl.

燴溜魚、
VELVET CHAMPAGNE FISH

Servings: 4 to 6   Cooking time: 8 minutes

1 cup water
5 tablespoons cornstarch
2 tablespoons whiskey
1 teaspoon sugar
1 pound fresh fish filets, cod or haddock
2 tablespoons plus 1 teaspoon vegetable oil
5 garlic cloves, thinly sliced
1 teaspoon salt
2 scallions, chopped

In small deep heatproof bowl mix together water, 2 tablespoons cornstarch, whiskey, and sugar. Cook on High 3 minutes and reserve.

Rinse filets in cold water and pat dry. Cut fish into 2-inch pieces and coat with remaining 3 tablespoons cornstarch. Let stand.

Add 1 teaspoon oil and garlic to large heatproof dish. Cook on High 1 minute. Add salt and stir. Remove and reserve garlic slices.

In same dish, place coated fish and add remaining oil. Toss to coat fish. Arrange fish evenly, leaving center open. Cook on High 2 minutes. Stir gently and cook on High 1 minute more.

Sprinkle reserved garlic slices over fish. Pour reserved cornstarch-whiskey sauce over fish and mix lightly. Cook on High 1 minute. Sprinkle chopped scallions over hot fish.

TIP
Velvet Champagne Fish is the traditional name for this dish although champagne is not actually used. In this case, the champagne is as figurative as the velvet.

蒜子蛤蜊或貼貝
SPICY STEAMED CLAMS OR MUSSELS

Servings: 4 to 6   Cooking time: 8 minutes

3 dozen fresh clams (or mussels) in shell
2 scallions, chopped
2 garlic cloves, minced
2 tablespoons soy sauce
1 tablespoon dry sherry
1 tablespoon vegetable oil
1 teaspoon cider or white vinegar
½ teaspoon hot red pepper (cayenne)
¼ teaspoon sugar

Scrub clams or mussels thoroughly, removing all sand. Scrape off beards from mussels. Arrange shellfish in large heatproof dish in single layer, leaving center open. (13 inches by 8 inches is a convenient size.)

Combine remaining ingredients and pour over shellfish. Cover with plastic wrap, leaving small vent. Steam on High 5 minutes. Give dish a quarter turn. Steam on High 3 minutes more, or until shells open.

TIPS
This dish may be served hot or cold.

To remove sand from clams or mussels, put them in enough highly salted cold water to cover, about 1 tablespoon salt per quart of water. Soak for 30 minutes. Drain off salted water and rinse well with cold water. Discard any clams or mussels with open shells.

雪豆蝦仁
SUCCULENT SHRIMP WITH SNOW PEAS

Servings: 4 to 6   Cooking time: 3½ minutes

1 pound raw shrimp, shelled and deveined, about 40
2 tablespoons plus ¼ teaspoon salt
2 thin slices ginger root, minced
2 tablespoons dry sherry
1 tablespoon plus ¼ teaspoon vegetable oil
1 cup snow peas, stems and strings removed
Cilantro (Chinese parsley) or watercress for garnish (optional)

Sprinkle 2 tablespoons salt over prepared shrimp and mix well. Rinse well in cold water to remove salt. Run very cold water over shrimp about 5 minutes. Drain. Dry shrimp thoroughly.

Mix shrimp with ginger, sherry, remaining ¼ teaspoon salt, and 1 tablespoon oil. Arrange shrimp in one layer in heatproof dish, leaving center open. Cook on High 1½ minutes. Sprinkle remaining ¼ teaspoon oil over snow peas and mix with shrimp. Arrange in one layer, leaving center open. Cook on High 2 minutes. Avoid overcooking. Shrimp should be plump and moist.

TIPS
Salting and rinsing shrimp in cold water firms the texture.

Larger shrimp may require slightly more cooking. Cook uncovered on High ½ minute at a time and test.

For frozen shrimp, see thawing directions in the manufacturer's manual for your microwave oven.

蒜爆蝦仁
STIR-FRIED SHRIMP WITH GARLIC

Servings: 4 to 6   Cooking time: 3½ minutes

2 tablespoons plus ¼ teaspoon salt
1 pound medium raw shrimp, shelled and deveined, about 40
2 to 3 garlic cloves, minced
2 thin slices ginger root, minced
2 tablespoons dry sherry
1 tablespoon vegetable oil
Cilantro (Chinese parsley) or watercress for garnish (optional)

Sprinkle 2 tablespoons salt over prepared shrimp and mix well. Rinse well in cold water to remove salt. Run very cold water over shrimp for about 5 minutes. Drain and dry thoroughly on paper towels.

Mix shrimp with garlic, ginger, sherry, ¼ teaspoon salt, and oil. Arrange shrimp in one layer in heatproof dish, leaving center open. Cook on High 2 minutes. Stir.

Rearrange shrimp in one layer, leaving center open. Cook on High 1½ minutes more. Avoid overcooking. Shrimp should be plump and moist.

TIPS
Vegetables, such as bamboo shoots, peas, blanched green beans, or scallions may be added in last minutes of cooking.

Salting and rinsing shrimp in cold water firms the texture.

Larger shrimp may require longer cooking. Cook, uncovered, on High ½ minute at a time and test for doneness.

For frozen shrimp, see thawing directions in the manufacturer's manual for your microwave oven.

清炒鮮貝
SHINY SCALLOPS

Servings: 4 to 6   Cooking time: 9 minutes

5 to 6 dried Chinese mushrooms
1 pound fresh scallops
¼ cup dry sherry
1 tablespoon dried shrimp
2 to 3 slices ginger root
1 tablespoon plus 1 teaspoon vegetable oil
½ teaspoon salt, or more to taste

Rinse mushrooms and place in 1-quart heatproof measure with 1 cup warm water. Cover with plastic wrap, leaving small vent. Heat on High 4 minutes. Let stand 5 minutes, in or out of oven. Remove hard stems and discard. Cut in ⅛-inch strips and reserve.

If scallops are small bay scallops, leave whole. Otherwise, cut in half. Marinate scallops in sherry 15 minutes, stirring from time to time. Drain off sherry and discard.

Rinse shrimp and soak in ½ cup warm water 10 minutes. Drain.

Place shrimp, mushrooms, and ginger in large shallow heatproof dish. Sprinkle with 1 tablespoon oil. Cook on High 1 minute. Remove ginger and discard.

Mix in scallops. Sprinkle with remaining oil and salt. Toss well with shrimp and mushrooms. Arrange in single layer, leaving center open. Cover, leaving small vent. Cook on High 2 minutes. Give dish a quarter turn. Cook on High 1 minute more. Let stand, covered, for 1 minute.

TIP
Always rinse dried mushrooms before soaking to remove small particles that can cause too much foaming when they are heated in water and result in overflow from the bowl.

豆豉生蠔
OYSTERS WITH BLACK BEAN SAUCE

Servings: 4 to 6   Cooking time: 4½ minutes

2 tablespoons vegetable oil
1 tablespoon minced fermented black beans
1 garlic clove, minced
1 slice ginger root, minced
12 ounces fresh oysters (approximately 30 medium sized), shucked
    and drained
1 tablespoon soy sauce
1 teaspoon dry sherry
1 tablespoon cornstarch

To a heatproof dish, add oil, black beans, garlic, and ginger. Cook on High 2 minutes. Stir. Add oysters, soy sauce, sherry, and cornstarch. Stir. Arrange oysters, leaving center open. Cook on High 1½ minutes. Stir. Rearrange, leaving center open. Give dish a quarter turn. Cook on High 1 minute more.

TIP
Fermented black beans are highly aromatic. When added to sauces, they blend in and mellow while enriching the flavor.

鍋貼一品虾
STUFFED SHRIMP

Servings: 4 to 6   Cooking time: 5 minutes

Stuffing (see below)
2 tablespoons plus ¼ teaspoon salt
12 large raw shrimp, shelled and deveined
Few drops sesame oil
Dash white pepper or Szechuan pepper
½ egg white, slightly beaten, (other ½ is used in stuffing)
Vegetable oil
Bread crumbs

Make stuffing and let stand 10 minutes. Divide stuffing into 12 equal portions and reserve.

Sprinkle 2 tablespoons salt over prepared shrimp and mix well. Rinse well in cold water and remove salt. Run very cold water over shrimp for about 5 minutes. Drain and dry thoroughly.

Butterfly shrimp by splitting lengthwise down the back, almost but not quite through. Take care to leave the two halves attached. Remove vein, rinse, and dry thoroughly. Put in bowl and add remaining ¼ teaspoon salt, sesame oil, and pepper. Mix gently. Add ½ egg white and mix. Let stand 5 minutes.

Place one portion reserved stuffing on each shrimp and mold lightly to cover. Arrange in heatproof dish in 1 layer, leaving center open. Brush shrimp with oil, sprinkle lightly with crumbs. Cook on High 3 minutes. Give dish a quarter turn, cook on High 2 minutes more.

STUFFING
4 ounces (about ½ cup) ground pork, not too lean
½ pound medium raw shrimp, shelled, deveined, and minced
6 water chestnuts, finely diced
2 tablespoons chopped scallions
1 tablespoon white flour
½ egg white
½ teaspoon salt
½ teaspoon sugar
½ teaspoon five-spice powder
½ teaspoon sesame oil
Dash white pepper

Mix all ingredients together and stir until almost a paste.

TIPS
Salting and rinsing shrimp in cold water firms the texture.

Larger shrimp may require slightly more cooking. Cook uncovered on High ½ minute at a time and test.

For frozen shrimp, see thawing directions in the manufacturer's manual for your microwave oven.

7 · EGGS

Imperial court records relate that one royal family and attendants consumed 400,000 eggs in one year. Chicken and duck eggs are the Chinese convenience foods, which are often salted, pickled, smoked, and hardcooked. The so-called hundred-year-old or thousand-year-old eggs are prepared in a few months. They are covered with a paste of lime, ash, and salt until the flavors have permeated and preserved the eggs. Tea eggs, a favorite snack, are hardcooked eggs steeped in spiced tea. When the shells are removed, the eggs have a handsomely marbled surface and a delicate spicy flavor.

Eggs figured in religious rites like the Festival of the Dead when villagers spent the day at the town cemetery honoring deceased relatives and friends. The customary lunch was duck eggs and pastries.

In a charming custom celebrating the birth of a son, the new father gives red-dyed eggs to relatives and friends. The color red is the symbol of happy and important events.

Popular dishes combine shrimp and crabmeat with eggs in omelets and custards. In the yin-yang philosophy crab is among the foods that have cold qualities whereas fried and spicy foods have hot qualities. In a healthy body the two elements are balanced but too much of either causes illness. Thus, fever can be cured by eating such "cold" foods as the crab omelet, included here, to restore balance.

Among the other dishes we have included in this chapter are scrambled eggs with black beans and an attractive meat-filled rolled egg sheet. You will find the recipe for Tea Eggs in Chapter 1.

We use hardcooked eggs in a few dishes, and you have a choice of the conventional or microwave method. We devised the first microwave recipe for hardcooking eggs (see page 91). Whichever method you use, put the cooked eggs immediately in cold running water. The cooling eggs shrink slightly so that the shells do not stick when the eggs are peeled.

金錢蛋

COIN EGGS WITH BEEF SAUCE

Servings: 4 to 6   Cooking time: 7 minutes

2 tablespoons soy sauce
2 tablespoons chopped scallions
2 teaspoons dry sherry
2 thin slices ginger root, minced (optional)
1 teaspoon cornstarch mixed with ½ cup water
2 teaspoons vegetable oil
2 garlic cloves, minced
½ pound finely ground beef
6 hardcooked eggs, peeled

Combine soy sauce, scallions, sherry, ginger, and cornstarch mixture for sauce. Reserve. Put oil and garlic in large heatproof glass pie plate. Heat on High 2 minutes. Add beef and garlic, and mix. Spread meat in even layer, leaving center open. Heat on High 1 to 2 minutes, or until meat shows no pink. Stir and break up meat. Add reserved sauce and combine with meat. Rearrange meat, leaving center open. Cook on High 2 minutes. Stir. Cook on High 1 minute more. Stir again.

Cut each egg crosswise into about 6 slices. Arrange in large dish, leaving center open. Pour meat sauce over egg slices. Cover with plastic wrap and cook on High 1 minute.

TIP
Eggs can be hardcooked in microwave oven (see page 91).

CRABMEAT OMELET

Servings: 4 to 6   Cooking time: 16 minutes

4 dried Chinese mushrooms
1 tablespoon plus 1 teaspoon vegetable oil
6 eggs, lightly beaten
1 small scallion, chopped
1 thin slice ginger, minced
4 water chestnuts, diced
1 teaspoon dry sherry
½ teaspoon salt
½ cup crabmeat, fresh, canned, or frozen

Rinse mushrooms, and place in 1-quart heatproof measure with 1 cup warm water. Cover with plastic wrap, leaving small vent. Heat on High 4 minutes. Let stand 5 minutes, inside or outside oven. Remove hard stems and discard. Cut in ⅛-inch strips. Reserve.

Coat 9-inch heatproof pie plate with 1 tablespoon oil, leaving excess oil in dish to prevent the eggs from sticking. Heat on High 4 minutes.

Mix together eggs, mushrooms, remaining 1 teaspoon oil, scallion, ginger, water chestnuts, sherry, salt, and crabmeat. Pour into heated dish. Cover, leaving small vent. Cook on Low 3 minutes. Using a spoon, push egg mixture from outer edge of dish to center to allow eggs in center to flow to outer edge. Give dish a quarter turn. Re-cover, leaving small vent. Cook on Low 2 minutes. Again, push eggs from outer edge of dish to center to allow eggs in center to flow to outer edge. Re-cover, leaving small vent. Cook on Low 2 minutes. Give dish a quarter turn. Re-cover, leaving small vent. Cook on Low 1 minute more. Let stand 5 minutes.

TIPS
Defrost frozen crabmeat before using.

Place dish off center during cooking to insure more even cooking.

Always rinse dried mushrooms before soaking to remove small particles that can cause too much foaming when they are heated in water and result in overflow from the bowl.

雞蛋肉餅
EGG FOO YONG

Servings: 4 to 6   Cooking time: 19 minutes

3 to 4 dried Chinese mushrooms (optional)
½ pound ground pork
½ teaspoon finely chopped ginger root
1 tablespoon chopped scallions
¼ teaspoon plus ¼ teaspoon salt
1 teaspoon dry sherry
1 tablespoon plus 1 teaspoon soy sauce
1 teaspoon sesame oil
6 eggs, slightly beaten
1 tablespoon vegetable oil

Rinse mushrooms, if used, and place in 1-quart heatproof measure with 1 cup warm water. Cover with plastic wrap, leaving small vent. Heat on High 4 minutes. Let stand 5 minutes, inside or outside oven. Remove hard stems and discard. Slice in ¼-inch strips and reserve.

To ground pork, add ginger, scallions, ¼ teaspoon salt, sherry, soy sauce, sesame oil, and mushrooms. Stir. Add eggs and stir. Add remaining ¼ teaspoon salt and stir again.

Use heatproof glass ring mold or large heatproof dish with small bowl in center as a spacer. Add vegetable oil. Heat on High 3 minutes. Pour in egg mixture. Cover with plastic wrap. Cook on Low 6 minutes. Give dish a quarter turn. Cook on Low 6 minutes more. Let stand, covered, for 2 minutes.

TIP
Always rinse dried mushrooms before soaking to remove small particles that can cause too much foaming when they are heated in water and result in overflow from the bowl.

STEAMED EGGS

Servings: 4 to 6   Cooking time: 12 minutes

Vegetable oil
6 large eggs, beaten
1 small scallion, finely chopped
2 teaspoons soy sauce
1 teaspoon dry sherry
1 cup chicken broth, homemade or canned

Coat glass ring mold well with oil. Mix together eggs, scallion, soy sauce, sherry, and broth. Pour egg mixture into oiled ring mold. Cook on Low 8 minutes. Give dish a quarter turn. Cook on High 3 minutes. Give dish a quarter turn. Cook on High 1 to 3 minutes more until the texture is custardlike.

TIPS
Texture of this dish is a soft yet firm custard, too delicate to unmold.

Glass ring mold is recommended to ensure even cooking. If ring mold not available, place small oiled bowl or cup in center of 8- to 9-inch-wide bowl.

蛋捲

ROLLED EGG DAINTIES

Servings: 4 to 6   Cooking time: 16 minutes

½ **pound finely ground pork**
1 **tablespoon dry sherry**
4 **teaspoons soy sauce**
1 **teaspoon minced ginger root**
½ **teaspoon sesame oil**
¼ **teaspoon salt**
¼ **teaspoon sugar**
1 **egg, unbeaten**
Vegetable oil
4 **eggs, well beaten**

Combine pork, sherry, soy sauce, ginger, sesame oil, salt, sugar, and the unbeaten egg and mix well. Reserve for stuffing.

Generously oil an 8¾-inch-by-13-inch heatproof dish. Heat on High 5 minutes. Pour beaten eggs into dish and distribute evenly. Cover with plastic wrap, leaving small vent. Cook on High 1 minute. Give dish a quarter turn and cook on High 1 minute more.

Carefully loosen egg sheet completely. Leave in dish. Spread stuffing evenly over egg sheet. Roll into a cylinder. Cover dish, leaving small vent. Cook on High 3 minutes. Give dish a quarter turn. Cook on High 6 minutes more. Cut into thin slices for serving.

滷蛋

SPICED EGGS IN MEAT SAUCE

Servings: 4 to 6   Cooking time: 2½ minutes

1 tablespoon fermented, salted black beans
¼ pound ground pork (about ½ cup)
2 tablespoons hoisin sauce
1 tablespoon soy sauce
1 tablespoon dry sherry
1 tablespoon chopped scallions
2 teaspoons minced garlic
1 thin slice ginger, minced
6 hardcooked eggs, shelled

Put beans and ½ cup water in heatproof 1-cup measure. Heat on High ½ minute, let stand 5 minutes, and drain. Chop beans coarsely and reserve.

Spread pork in even layer in heatproof pie plate, cook on High 1 minute, or until pork shows no pink. Drain off juices and break up clumps of pork. Combine pork and beans with rest of ingredients, except eggs, and mix well.

Cut eggs in lengthwise halves and spread meat mixture on each half. Put egg halves in heatproof pie plate, leaving center open, and cover with plastic wrap. Cook on High 1 minute.

TIP
Eggs can be hardcooked in microwave oven (see page 91).

SALTY EGGS

Servings: 4 to 6   Cooking time: 4 minutes

2 cups water
⅛ cup salt
1 tablespoon whole peppercorns
2 tablespoons dry sherry
6 raw eggs in shell

To 1-quart heatproof bowl add 2 cups water, salt, and peppercorns. Cover, leaving small vent. Heat on High 4 minutes. Stir and let cool to room temperature. Add sherry. Pour mixture into screw cap jar. Carefully place eggs in jar, one at a time. Salt water mixture must cover eggs. Screw cap on tightly. Keep eggs at room temperature 1 month.

At end of a month, finish cooking by hardcooking as you would any raw eggs. Peel, then quarter or slice eggs for garnish or as a relish with hot rice.

TIPS
Raw eggs marinated in salt water at room temperature for 1 month will not spoil provided the liquid level is above the eggs.

Eggs can be hardcooked in microwave oven (see page 91).

SCRAMBLED EGGS WITH BLACK BEANS

Servings: 4 to 6   Cooking time: 9½ minutes

2 teaspoons fermented, salted black beans
4 teaspoons vegetable oil
6 eggs, well beaten but not frothy
1 tablespoon chopped scallions
1 tablespoon soy sauce
1 teaspoon dry sherry

Put beans and ½ cup water in 1-cup heatproof measure. Heat on High ½ minute, let stand for 5 minutes, and drain. Chop beans coarsely and reserve.

Coat 2-quart heatproof bowl generously with oil, leaving excess oil in bowl. Add eggs to bowl. Place bowl away from center of oven. Cook on Low 6 minutes. Add beans, scallions, soy sauce, and sherry. Stir gently. Cook on Low 2 minutes. Cover tightly with plastic wrap. Cook on High 1 minute. Stir well. Re-cover. Let stand 2 minutes.

TIPS

In all cooking steps place bowl away from center of oven to aid cooking of eggs in center of bowl.

Finished eggs should be moist and tender.

HARDCOOKED EGGS

Servings: 4 to 6   Cooking time: 18 minutes

1 teaspoon salt
4 cups warm water
6 eggs

Put salt and water in heatproof 2-quart bowl and cover with plastic wrap, leaving small vent. Heat on High 7 to 8 minutes, or until water begins to boil.

Lower eggs carefully, one at a time, into hot water. Re-cover, vent, and let eggs stand 5 minutes.

Cook on High 3½ minutes and give bowl a quarter turn. Cook on High 6½ minutes more.

Cool eggs immediately in cold running water. Remove shells.

TIPS

Use caution when lifting cover because of buildup of hot steam.

Immediate cooling of cooked eggs prevents shells from sticking when eggs are peeled.

8 · VEGETABLES

In Chinese meals vegetables when combined with small portions of meat are called *tsai* and they embellish the main dish of grain called *fan*. Locally grown vegetables impart characteristic flavors to regional cooking. In the north, cold-resistant and root vegetables, celery cabbage, bok choy with white branches and dark green leaves, and the compact European cabbage are basic to their dishes. The European carrot has replaced the fibrous native variety, but the large Chinese radish is still cultivated. Vegetables are pickled and salted for use during the long bitter winters.

Ginger root, garlic, bamboo shoots, green onions, and mushrooms are universally used. Ginger root, once believed to increase fertility, imparts a subtle Chinese flavor to dishes. Special varieties of bamboo, symbol of nobility, were nurtured in the imperial Tang gardens for the royal kitchen. Green onions, or scallions, were once thought to ease minor winter illnesses. Many kinds of fungi flourish: cloud ears; silver ears; black mushrooms, which grow wild; and the cultivated straw mushroom. Dried Chinese mushrooms are expensive but, like the French truffle, impart a special flavor when used sparingly. We have included a recipe using straw mushrooms in this chapter. You will find three mushroom dishes in Chapter 1, and a mushroom sauce in Chapter 10.

Many imported vegetables were absorbed into Chinese cooking such as South American peanuts, corn, sweet potatoes, tropical eggplant, pistachio nuts from the Middle East, and the European garden pea. Hot chili peppers from India were welcomed into Szechuan dishes already spicy with the native fagara or brown pepper. All these and many other foods have been assimilated, but Chinese cooking retains a character uniquely its own.

ASPARAGUS SALAD

Servings: 4 to 6   Cooking time: 3 minutes

1 pound fresh asparagus
2 teaspoons vegetable oil
½ teaspoon salt
½ teaspoon sugar
1 teaspoon soy sauce
½ teaspoon water

Cut off tough ends of asparagus and discard. Cut remainder of stalks into 1½-inch lengths.

Place asparagus in heatproof glass pie plate. Add oil, salt, sugar, soy sauce, and water. Stir. Cover with plastic wrap, leaving small vent. Cook on High 2 minutes. Give dish a quarter turn. Cook on High 1 minute. Serve hot or cold.

BEAN SPROUTS WITH CUCUMBER STRIPS

Servings: 4 to 6   Cooking time: 8 minutes

½ pound bean sprouts
1 cucumber
5 dried Chinese mushrooms
1 tablespoon vegetable oil
½ teaspoon salt, or to taste
¼ teaspoon sesame oil

Rinse bean sprouts and drain. Cut unpeeled cucumber in ¼-inch slices, then in thin strips.

Rinse mushrooms, and place in 1-quart heatproof measure with 1 cup water. Cover with plastic wrap, leaving small vent. Heat on High 4 minutes. Let stand 5 minutes, inside or outside oven. Remove hard stems and discard. Cut in thin strips and place in large heatproof dish with oil. Cover, leaving small vent. Cook on High 2 minutes. Mix in bean sprouts and cucumber. Cook on High 2 minutes more. Drain off liquid. Add salt to taste. Sprinkle with sesame oil. Mix well.

TIP
Always rinse dried mushrooms before soaking to remove small particles that can cause too much foaming when they are heated in water and result in overflow from the bowl.

炒三鮮

STIR-FRIED BEAN SPROUTS, SNOW PEAS, AND BAMBOO SHOOTS

Servings: 4 to 6   Cooking time: 4 minutes

1 cup bean sprouts, fresh or canned
1 cup snow peas
1 cup canned bamboo shoots
1 tablespoon vegetable oil
1 teaspoon salt

If using canned bean sprouts, rinse in cold water, drain well, and dry.

Remove stems and strings from snow peas. Drain bamboo shoots, cut in ¼-inch-thick slices, then in 1-inch-long strips.

Mix vegetables together, sprinkle with oil and salt, and toss. Spread in even layer in large heatproof dish, leaving center open. Cook on High 3 minutes, and stir. Spread in even layer, leaving center open. Cook on High 1 minute more, and stir.

TIP
Vegetables should be cooked but crisp.

炒白菜
SHIMMERY BOK CHOY

Servings: 4 to 6   Cooking time: 3 minutes

1 pound bok choy
2 tablespoons vegetable oil
¼ teaspoon salt

Cut bok choy diagonally in 1-inch slices, add oil, and toss to mix. Arrange in even layer in large heatproof dish, leaving center open. Sprinkle salt over bok choy. Cook on High 3 minutes.

TIP
This dish may be served with Szechuan Pork (page 58), Pearl Meatballs (page 22), or Sesame Pork Tenderloin (page 54).

清炒芥兰
STIR-FRIED BROCCOLI

Servings: 4 to 6   Cooking time: 4 minutes

1 bunch fresh broccoli
1 tablespoon vegetable oil
1 tablespoon water
1 teaspoon salt

Cut off large broccoli flowerets and divide into smaller pieces. Slice stem lengthwise in quarters, then in ½-inch long pieces. Sprinkle broccoli with oil, water, salt, and toss. Spread in even layer in large heatproof dish, leaving center open. Cover with plastic wrap, leaving small vent. Cook on High 2 minutes and give dish a quarter turn. Cook on High 2 minutes more.

TIP
Broccoli should be cooked but still crisp.

Bao Tze and Won Ton Soup seen against the Great Wall.

Oyster Sauce Beef with Broccoli, White Cut Chicken, Hot Chili Paste, and Cooked Soy Dip with the Gweilin peaks in the background.

Steamed Fish in Black Bean Sauce on the shore of the West Lake in Hangchow.

Red-cooked Duck and Tea Eggs in front of the famous Marble Boat in Beijing.

白菜豆腐
SIMMERED CABBAGE AND TOFU

Servings: 4 to 6   Cooking time: 12 minutes

1 pound celery cabbage
1 tablespoon vegetable oil
1 cup chicken broth, homemade or canned
Salt to taste
½ pound tofu (bean curd)
¼ teaspoon sesame oil (optional)

Cut cabbage lengthwise in ½-inch-wide sections, then crosswise in 1-inch chunks. Sprinkle with oil and toss to coat. Spread in even layer in large heatproof dish, leaving center open. Cover with plastic wrap and cook on High 2 minutes. Add broth, taste for salt, and reserve.

Drain tofu, cut in ¼-inch-thick slices, then in 1-inch squares. Sprinkle with sesame oil and mix gently. Add tofu to cabbage, toss lightly, and cover with plastic wrap. Cook on High 5 minutes and give dish a quarter turn. Cook on High 5 minutes more.

TIPS
Cabbage should be cooked but firm.

Canned broth tends to be saltier than homemade, so taste before adding salt.

豆豉蘿蔔丁

CARROTS WITH GARLIC AND BLACK BEANS

Servings: 4 to 6   Cooking time: 11 minutes

2 cups diced carrots (about 8 medium-size carrots)
5 tablespoons water
1 tablespoon vegetable oil
1 garlic clove, minced (about 1 teaspoon)
1 teaspoon minced, fermented black beans
1 tablespoon soy sauce

Place carrots in heatproof dish in even layer, leaving center open. Add 2 tablespoons water. Cover. Cook on High 4 minutes. Drain and reserve.

To large heatproof dish add oil, garlic, and black beans. Cook on High 2 minutes. Add reserved carrots and stir well. Add 3 tablespoons water and soy sauce to carrots. Cook on High 3 minutes. Give dish a quarter turn. Stir. Cook on High 2 minutes. Stir, let stand 5 minutes.

乾炒香茄

GARLIC-SCENTED EGGPLANT

Servings: 4 to 6   Cooking time: 8 minutes

1 tablespoon vegetable oil
1 large eggplant, peeled, cut in small cubes
3 to 5 garlic cloves, chopped
¼ cup soy sauce
1 tablespoon sugar
1 teaspoon salt

Add oil to eggplant, and stir. Arrange in even layer in heatproof dish, leaving center open. Cover with plastic wrap, leaving small vent. Cook on High 2 minutes. Give dish a quarter turn. Cook on High 2 minutes more.

Mix together garlic, soy sauce, sugar, and salt. Pour over eggplant. Re-cover, leaving small vent. Cook on High 2 minutes. Give dish a quarter turn. Cook on High 2 minutes more. Cool and chill. Serve cold.

糖醋青椒

SWEET-AND-SOUR GREEN PEPPERS AND WALNUTS

Servings: 4 to 6   Cooking time: 13½ minutes

¼ cup cider or white vinegar
6 tablespoons sugar
1 tablespoon ketchup
1 tablespoon soy sauce
4½ teaspoons cornstarch mixed with ½ cup water
1 small yellow onion, peeled
2 green peppers
1 cup walnut meats
1 tablespoon vegetable oil

Combine vinegar, sugar, ketchup, soy sauce, and cornstarch mixture in small deep heatproof bowl. Cook on High 4 minutes. Reserve sauce.

Cut onion in ¼-inch slices; separate into rings. Remove seeds from green pepper, cut in ¼-inch slices.

Arrange walnuts in even layer in heatproof dish, leaving center open. Heat on High 3 minutes. Give dish a quarter turn. Heat on High 1 minute. Reserve walnuts.

Add oil to large heatproof dish. Heat on High 3 minutes. Add onion and pepper slices and stir. Cook on High 2 minutes. Add reserved sauce and stir. Cook on High ½ minute more. Add walnuts and stir. Serve.

蠔油草菇

STRAW MUSHROOMS IN OYSTER SAUCE

Servings: 4 to 6   Cooking time: 5 minutes

1 15-ounce can Chinese straw mushrooms
¼ cup water
2 tablespoons oyster sauce
1 tablespoon cornstarch
Salt to taste

Drain mushrooms and discard liquid. Spread mushrooms in even layer in heatproof pie plate, leaving center open.

Combine water, oyster sauce, and cornstarch. Pour over mushrooms, cook on High 3 minutes, and give dish a quarter turn. Cook on High 2 minutes, or until sauce thickens. Stir. Taste before adding salt.

炒洋絲瓜

STIR-FRIED ZUCCHINI WITH GARLIC

Servings: 4 to 6   Cooking time: 7 minutes

1 1-pound zucchini, unpeeled
2 teaspoons dry sherry
½ teaspoon salt
2 tablespoons vegetable oil
3 garlic cloves, minced

Cut zucchini lengthwise in quarters, then in ¼-inch-thick slices. Sprinkle with sherry and salt.

Add oil and garlic to large heatproof dish and cook on High 3 minutes. Add zucchini, stir, and cover with plastic wrap, leaving small vent. Cook on High 2 minutes. Stir, re-cover, and vent. Cook on High 2 minutes more and let stand covered 5 minutes.

TIP
Zucchini should be cooked but firm.

TOFU CASSEROLE

Servings: 4 to 6   Cooking time: 6 minutes

1 pound tofu (bean curd)
3 tablespoons soy sauce
1 tablespoon dry sherry
2 teaspoons chopped, fermented, salted black beans
1 teaspoon cornstarch mixed with 1 tablespoon water
½ teaspoon sugar
¼ pound thinly sliced pork (about ½ cup)
1 tablespoon vegetable oil

Drain tofu, squeeze lightly, and pat dry. Cut in ½-inch-thick slices, then in 2-inch squares. Reserve.

Combine 2 tablespoons soy sauce, sherry, black beans, cornstarch mixture, and sugar. Pour over pork and mix well. Add oil to large heatproof dish, spread pork in even layer, leaving center open. Cook on High 3 minutes, and stir. Spread in even layer, leaving center open. Cook on High 1 minute more, and stir.

Drain off and discard liquid from reserved tofu. Mix with pork, sprinkle with remaining soy sauce, cover with plastic wrap, and cook on High 2 minutes, or until warm.

涼拌豆腐

TOFU AND PEANUT SALAD

Servings: 4 to 6   Cooking time: 16 minutes

1 pound tofu (bean curd), diced
2 cups water
2 teaspoons sesame oil
1 cup Spiced Szechuan Peanuts (see page 27)
Salt to taste

Put tofu and water in 1-quart heatproof bowl, cover with plastic wrap, leaving small vent. Cook on High 5 minutes and give bowl a quarter turn. Cook on High 3 minutes, or until water begins to bubble. Drain and let tofu cool to room temperature.

Sprinkle with sesame oil and mix gently. Add peanuts and toss lightly. Taste before adding salt. Chill well before serving.

TIPS

Cooking time includes preparation of peanuts. They are salty, so taste before adding salt to salad.

Tofu has a delicate texture and breaks up easily. Careful handling is recommended. Simmering firms the tofu somewhat.

VEGETARIAN'S DELIGHT

Servings: 4 to 6   Cooking time: 11 minutes

2 tablespoons vegetable oil
3 eggs, well beaten
1 ounce cellophane noodles (optional)
3 dried Chinese mushrooms
1 tablespoon dried shrimp (optional)
1 cup chopped bean sprouts
1 cup chopped fresh mushrooms
½ teaspoon sesame oil (optional)
Salt to taste

Coat 1-quart heatproof bowl generously with 1 tablespoon oil, add eggs, cover with plastic wrap. Cook on High 1 minute, and stir. Re-cover, cook on High 1 minute more. Stir and reserve. Scrambled eggs should be dry and fluffy.

Rinse noodles in water, put in 1-quart heatproof measure with 2 cups water, and cook on High 4 minutes. Drain, rinse with cold water, chop, and reserve.

Rinse dried mushrooms and shrimp in cold water, put in 1-quart heatproof measure with 2 cups water, and cover with plastic wrap, leaving small vent. Heat on High 4 minutes. Let stand 5 minutes, and drain. Discard hard stems of mushrooms, chop mushrooms and shrimps, and reserve.

Break up clumps of scrambled eggs, add noodles, mushroom mixture, bean sprouts, fresh mushrooms, and mix well. Sprinkle with remaining vegetable oil and sesame oil, and toss. Taste before adding salt. Heat on High 1 minute or until warm.

TIPS

Vegetarian's Delight can be served as a meatless main dish.

Always rinse dried mushrooms in water to remove small particles that can cause too much foaming when they are heated in water and result in overflow from the bowl.

Rinse dried shrimp in water to remove small particles that can cause too much foaming when they are heated in water and result in overflow from the bowl.

9 · SIDE DISHES

Grain dishes, *fan*, are the mainstay of Chinese meals. Strictly translated, fan means rice but includes breads and buns, dumplings, noodles (*mein*), and pancakes (*ping*). The regional use of certain grains is related to the local climate. Hundreds of varieties of rice—long and short grain, glutinous or sweet, red, yellow, and black— are grown in the warm fertile south. When eating rice in China, the polite diner raises his rice bowl to his face and pushes the rice to his mouth with chopsticks. Lifting a chopstickful of rice from table level suggests displeasure with the food.

We have included at the end of this chapter basic recipes for preparation of several kinds of rice, including long, and short grain rice, and glutinous, or sweet, rice, an ingredient in such dishes as Pearl Meatballs and Jewel Pudding.

The major crops of cold northern China were sorghum, millet, and soy bean until the development of hardy strains of cold-resistant wheat, which mature rapidly in the short growing season. With modern irrigation, rice is grown as far north as Manchuria, but northerners prefer steamed breads and dumplings. The sweet potato, although not a grain, is considered *fan*. They are often roasted for snacks.

Noodles and stuffings wrapped in noodles or dough are common to both regions. The Cantonese relish egg noodles. The unusual thin cellophane noodle is made from mung beans and added to many dishes. Special dumplings like Chiao Tze marked the New Year and sugary coiled cakes the fall festival. Similar meat-filled dumplings are made in Russia and other central Asian countries bordering on China. In this chapter we have included four rice and noodle dishes. In Chapter 1, you will find recipes for several stuffed noodles and doughs. In Chapter 11 is a recipe for a sweet bean paste stuffed dough made from rice flour.

雞片炒麵

CHICKEN CHOW MEIN

Servings: 4 to 6   Cooking time: 33 minutes

1½ teaspoon salt
½ pound dried Chinese egg noodles
3 tablespoons vegetable oil
½ pound raw boneless chicken breast
1 tablespoon soy sauce
1 teaspoon dry sherry
1 teaspoon salt
¼ teaspoon white pepper
1 tablespoon cornstarch
2 cups bok choy
3 to 4 dried Chinese mushrooms

Add ½ teaspoon salt to 4 cups water in a heatproof 2-quart bowl. Cover with plastic wrap, leaving small vent. Put in corner of oven, and heat on High 7 to 9 minutes or until boiling. Add noodles, stir, re-cover, vent, and cook on High 2 minutes. Stir, re-cover, vent, cook on High 2 minutes more. Drain.

Add 2 tablespoons oil to large heatproof dish and heat on High 3 minutes. Spread noodles in even layer and heat on High 4 minutes. Turn over noodle layer and reserve.

Cut chicken breast across grain in ¼-inch-thick slices. Mix soy sauce, sherry, remaining teaspoon salt, pepper, and cornstarch. Add to chicken, mix, and reserve.

Cut cabbage diagonally in 1-inch-wide slices and reserve.

Rinse mushrooms in cold water, put in heatproof 1-quart measure with 1 cup water, and cover with plastic wrap, leaving small vent. Heat on High 4 minutes, let stand 5 minutes, and drain. Discard hard stems, cut mushrooms in ¼-inch-thick slices. Mix together mushrooms, bok choy, and remaining 1 tablespoon oil, and spread in even layer in large heatproof dish, leaving center open. Cook on High 4 minutes. Remove from dish, and reserve.

In same dish, spread chicken in even layer. Leaving center open, cook on High 2 minutes, and stir. Spread evenly, leaving center open, and cook 1 minute more. Combine bok choy mixture with chicken and pour over noodles. Do not mix. Heat on High 2 minutes or until noodles are warm.

TIPS
Use caution when lifting cover to stir or drain noodles because of buildup of hot steam.

Japanese-style alimentary paste noodles can be substituted for Chinese dried egg noodles.

Always rinse dried mushrooms to remove small particles that can cause too much foaming when they are heated in water and result in overflow from the bowl.

火腿炒飯
FRIED RICE WITH HAM

Servings: 6 to 10   Cooking time: 6 minutes

3 eggs
¾ teaspoon salt
2 tablespoons plus 1 teaspoon vegetable oil
3 cups cooked rice
½ cup chopped cooked ham
3 tablespoons cooked green peas
⅓ cup chopped scallions

Beat eggs lightly with ¼ teaspoon salt. Heat 1 teaspoon oil in large heatproof dish on High 1 minute. Add eggs, cook on High 1 minute, and stir. Cook on High 1 minute more.

Stir in rice. Add ham, peas, remaining ½ teaspoon salt and remaining 2 tablespoons oil, and mix well. Heat on High 2 to 3 minutes or until rice is hot. Sprinkle scallions over rice mixture.

TIPS
Pork, shrimp, and other leftover meats can be substituted for ham. Broccoli, green beans, and other leftover vegetables can be substituted for peas.

Can be served as a main dish.

肉絲白菜麵

NOODLES WITH PORK AND CABBAGE

Servings: 4 to 6   Cooking time: 20 minutes

4 tablespoons soy sauce
1 tablespoon dry sherry
1 tablespoon plus ½ teaspoon vegetable oil
1 teaspoon cornstarch
½ teaspoon sugar
½ teaspoon salt
1 slice ginger, cut in thin strips
¼ pound thinly sliced pork (about ½ cup)
3 cups cabbage
½ pound fresh soft Chinese noodles
4 tablespoons water

Combine 2 tablespoons soy sauce, sherry, 1 tablespoon oil, ginger, cornstarch, sugar, and ¼ teaspoon salt. Add pork and marinate 10 minutes. Cut cabbage across grain in ¼-inch-wide slices. Reserve.

Add remaining ¼ teaspoon salt and remaining ½ teaspoon oil, and 6 cups water to 3-quart heatproof bowl. Put in corner of oven, and heat on High 8 minutes. Add noodles, stir, and cook on High 4 minutes. Cover with plastic wrap, let stand 3 minutes. Drain, rinse in cold water, and reserve.

Spread pork in even layer in large heatproof dish, leaving center open. Cook on High 1 minute, and stir. Mix in cabbage, spread evenly, leaving center open. Cover with plastic wrap, leaving small vent. Cook on High 3 minutes and give dish a quarter turn. Cook on High 2 minutes more. Sprinkle with remaining 2 tablespoons soy sauce and stir. Sprinkle with 4 tablespoons water and mix well.

Spread noodles in large heatproof dish. Pour cabbage mixture over top. Do not mix. Heat on Low 2 minutes or until noodles are warm.

TIPS

Use caution when draining noodles because of buildup of steam.

Noodles should be cooked but firm. Cabbage should be soft but not mushy. Can be served as main dish.

香腸炒飯
FRIED RICE WITH CHINESE SAUSAGE

Servings: 4 to 6   Cooking time: 6 minutes

3 small Chinese sausages (about ¼ pound)
3 peeled carrots
3 tablespoons water
1 cup cooked rice
1 tablespoon vegetable oil
½ teaspoon salt

Put whole sausages and carrots in heatproof pie plate, leaving center open. Add water and cover tightly with plastic wrap. Cook on High 4 minutes, let cool, and dice. Combine sausage, carrots, rice, oil, and salt. Spread in even layer in heatproof pie plate. Heat on High 1 to 2 minutes or until rice is hot.

TIPS
Can be served as a main dish.
   Italian pepperoni or Spanish chorizo can be substituted for Chinese sausage.

糯米飯
GLUTINOUS RICE (SWEET RICE)

Servings: 4 to 6   Cooking time: 27 minutes

1 cup raw glutinous rice
1 teaspoon vegetable oil
½ teaspoon salt
4 cups water

Rinse rice several times in cold water. Put in heatproof 2-quart bowl, add oil, and stir to coat grains. Add salt, water, and stir. Cover with plastic wrap, leaving small vent, and put in corner of oven. Cook on High 6 minutes and stir. Give bowl a quarter turn, re-cover, and vent. Cook on High 6 minutes more, stir, re-cover, and vent. Cook on High 5 minutes and drain. Spread rice evenly in dish, leaving center open. Cover with plastic wrap, leaving small vent. Cook on Low 10 minutes.

TIPS
Use caution when lifting cover to stir or drain rice because of buildup of hot steam.

The cooked grains of glutinous rice cling together as the name implies.

Glutinous Rice is used only for stuffings and desserts and not served with meals as regular rice.

長米白飯
LONG GRAIN RICE

Servings: 4 to 6   Cooking time: 27 minutes

1 cup raw long grain rice
1 teaspoon vegetable oil
½ teaspoon salt
4 cups water

Rinse rice several times in cold water. Put in heatproof 2-quart bowl, add oil, and stir to coat grains. Add salt, water, and stir. Cover with plastic wrap, leaving small vent, and put in corner of oven. Cook on High 6 minutes and stir. Give bowl a quarter turn, re-cover, and vent. Cook on High 6 minutes more, stir, re-cover, and vent. Cook on High 5 minutes. Drain and rinse with cold water. Drain again. Place rice evenly in dish, leaving center open. Cover with plastic wrap, leaving small vent. Cook on Low 10 minutes. Serve hot.

TIPS
Use caution when lifting cover to stir or drain rice because of buildup of hot steam.

短米白飯
SHORT GRAIN RICE

Servings: 4 to 6   Cooking time: 27 minutes

1 cup raw short grain rice
1 teaspoon vegetable oil
½ teaspoon salt
4 cups water

Rinse rice several times in cold water. Put in heatproof 2-quart bowl, add oil, and stir to coat grains. Add salt, water, and stir. Cover with plastic wrap, leaving small vent, and put in corner of oven. Cook on High 6 minutes and stir. Give bowl a quarter turn, re-cover, and vent. Cook on High 6 minutes more, stir, re-cover, and vent. Cook on High 5 minutes. Drain and rinse with cold water. Drain again. Place rice evenly in dish, leaving center open. Cover with plastic wrap, leaving small vent. Cook on Low 10 minutes. Serve hot.

TIPS
Use caution when lifting cover to stir or drain rice because of buildup of hot steam.
Short grain rice is the best substitute for glutinous rice.

QUICK COOKING RICE

Servings: 4 to 6   Cooking time: 6 minutes

1¼ cups raw quick cooking rice
½ teaspoon vegetable oil
½ teaspoon salt
1¼ cups water

Put rice in heatproof 2-quart bowl, add oil, and stir to coat grains. Add salt, water, and stir. Put in corner of oven, cook on High 4 minutes, and stir. Cook on High 2 minutes more and stir. If rice is not completely cooked, let stand 3 to 5 minutes until all the water is absorbed.

TIP
A cover is not needed during cooking.

COLD COOKED RICE

Servings: 6 to 8   Warming time: 2 to 3 minutes

4 to 5 cups refrigerated cooked rice

Put rice in heatproof 2-quart bowl, cover with plastic wrap, and heat on High 2 to 3 minutes or until rice is warm.

FROZEN COOKED RICE

Servings: 6 to 8   Warming time: 10 minutes

4 to 5 cups frozen cooked rice

Put rice in heatproof 2-quart bowl, cover with plastic wrap, and heat on Low 5 minutes. Give bowl a quarter turn and heat on High 5 minutes or until rice is warm.

10 · DIPS, SAUCES, AND CONDIMENTS

Chinese dips and sauces add verve and diversity to many foods. The difference between the two is often a matter of use. For example, crispy fried Won Ton are dipped in a sweet-and-sour sauce but not served in the sauce, which would make them soggy. The same sauce is cooked with steamed fish and becomes part of the final dish. Dips, sauces, and condiments are meant to enhance foods but never to overwhelm the basic flavors.

We have included in this chapter several easy, inexpensive recipes for commercial Chinese products not usually stocked in supermarkets, such as hot and spicy oils, chili pastes, and five-spice powder. For your convenience, we have also provided several types of sauces, noting the foods that they complement. A simple stir-fried or steamed food can be turned into an elegant dish with the appropriate sauce. Since the volumes are small, the bowl or measure should be put away from the center of the microwave oven for even, rapid cooking.

MUSTARD DIP

Quantity: 6 tablespoons   Cooking time: ½ minute

3 tablespoons dry mustard
3 tablespoons water

Put mustard in heatproof 1-cup measure, add water, and stir to smooth paste. Cover with plastic wrap, leaving small vent, and place off center in oven. Heat on High ½ minute and stir well. Cool to room temperature. Refrigerate at least 1 hour to mellow flavor.

TIPS
Leftover dip may be stored several months refrigerated in tightly capped container.
　　Heating mixture helps mustard powder absorb water.

COOKED SOY DIP

Quantity: ½ cup   Cooking time: 1 minute

2 scallions, chopped
4 thin slices ginger root, minced
6 tablespoons soy sauce
1 teaspoon vegetable oil
½ teaspoon dry sherry
½ teaspoon sugar

Put all ingredients in heatproof 2-cup measure, stir, and cook on High 1 minute. Serve either warm or cold. Dip can be stored several days covered and refrigerated.

辣汁
SOY AND CHILI DIP

Quantity: 6 tablespoons   Uncooked

6 tablespoons soy sauce
1 teaspoon sesame oil
1 teaspoon hot chili paste or more to taste
½ teaspoon sugar

Mix all ingredients together. Dip can be stored several days covered and refrigerated.

蒜汁
SOY AND GARLIC DIP

Quantity: ½ cup   Uncooked

2 scallions, chopped
2 garlic cloves, minced
6 tablespoons soy sauce
1 tablespoon vinegar
1 teaspoon sesame oil (optional)
½ teaspoon sugar

Mix all ingredients together. Dip can be stored several days covered and refrigerated.

生薑汁
SOY AND GINGER DIP

Quantity: 7 tablespoons   Uncooked

6 tablespoons soy sauce
1 tablespoon vinegar
1 teaspoon sugar
2 thin slices ginger root, minced

Mix all ingredients together. Dip can be stored several days covered and refrigerated.

醬油醋汁
SOY AND VINEGAR DIP

Quantity: ½ cup   Uncooked

4 tablespoons soy sauce
4 tablespoons vinegar
Few drops hot chili oil or Tabasco sauce to taste

Mix all ingredients together. Dip can be stored several weeks covered and refrigerated.

牛肉汁
BEEF SAUCE

Quantity: 1¼ cups   Cooking time: 8 minutes

1 garlic clove, minced
1 teaspoon vegetable oil
¼ pound finely ground beef (about ½ cup)
2 tablespoons chopped scallions
1 thin slice ginger root, minced

2 tablespoons soy sauce
2 teaspoons dry sherry
1 teaspoon cornstarch mixed with ½ cup water

Put garlic and oil in heatproof pie plate, cook on High 2 minutes. Mix in beef, spread in even layer, leaving center open. Cook on High 1 to 2 minutes or until beef shows no pink. Stir, and break up clumps.

Combine rest of ingredients, add to beef, and mix well. Spread in even layer, leaving center open. Cook on High 2 minutes, and stir. Cook on High 2 minutes more and stir.

TIP
Serve on eggs, noodles, and vegetables.

豆豉醬

BLACK BEAN SAUCE

Quantity: ½ cup   Cooking time: 3½ minutes

1 tablespoon fermented, salted black beans
½ cup water
3 tablespoons soy sauce
3 tablespoons dry sherry
1 tablespoon vegetable oil

Put beans and water in heatproof 1-cup measure. Heat on High ½ minute. Let stand 5 minutes, and drain. Chop beans coarsely.

Mix beans with rest of ingredients, put in heatproof 1-cup measure, cover with plastic wrap, and cook on High 3 minutes. Sauce can be stored several days tightly capped and refrigerated.

TIP
Black bean sauce goes well on eggs and vegetables.

豆豉肉醬
BLACK BEAN SAUCE WITH PORK

Quantity: 1 cup   Cooking time: 3½ minutes

1 tablespoon fermented, salted black beans
½ cup water
¼ pound finely ground pork (about ½ cup)
2 tablespoons hoisin sauce
1 tablespoon chopped scallions
1 tablespoon soy sauce
1 tablespoon dry sherry
2 teaspoons minced garlic
1 thin slice ginger root, minced

Put beans and water in heatproof 1-cup measure. Heat on High ½ minute, let stand 5 minutes, and drain. Chop coarsely and reserve.

Spread pork in heatproof pie plate in even layer, leaving center open. Cook on High 1 to 2 minutes or until pork shows no pink. Stir and break up clumps. Add rest of ingredients to pork, mix well, and cover with plastic wrap. Cook on High 1 minute, stir.

TIP
Black bean sauce with pork makes an excellent dish when poured over cooked noodles, eggs, or vegetables.

辣豆豉醬
HOT BLACK BEAN SAUCE

Quantity: ½ cup   Cooking time: 4½ minutes

2 teaspoons fermented, salted black beans
½ cup water
4 tablespoons chicken broth, homemade or canned
2 tablespoons soy sauce
2 tablespoons hoisin sauce
2 teaspoons ketchup

1 teaspoon sesame oil
1 teaspoon sugar
½ teaspoon hot chili paste, or dried crushed red pepper, or more to
    taste

Put beans and water in heatproof 1-cup measure. Heat on High ½ minute, let stand 5 minutes, and drain. Chop coarsely.

Mix beans with rest of ingredients, put in heatproof 2-cup measure, and cover with plastic wrap. Cook on High 2 minutes, stir, and re-cover. Cook on High 2 minutes more and stir. Sauce can be stored several days tightly capped and refrigerated.

TIP
This version of black bean sauce is very good with meats.

四川辣肉醬
SZECHUAN-STYLE CHILI SAUCE

Quantity: ½ cup   Cooking time: 2 minutes

3 tablespoons soy sauce
2 tablespoons dry sherry
1 tablespoon vegetable oil
1 teaspoon cornstarch mixed with 2 tablespoons water
2 to 3 slices ginger root, finely chopped
½ teaspoon hot chili paste or more to taste

Put all ingredients in heatproof 2-cup measure, stir, and cook on High 2 minutes. Dip can be stored several days covered and refrigerated.

TIP
Sauce is good with meats and hearty vegetables like cabbage, eggplant, and carrots.

奶油菜汁

CREAM SAUCE

Quantity: 1 cup   Cooking time: 7 minutes

1 tablespoon chopped scallions
1 teaspoon vegetable oil
½ cup chicken broth, homemade or canned
1 tablespoon cornstarch
½ cup milk or light cream
Salt to taste

Put scallions and oil in heatproof 2-quart bowl, and cook on High 2 minutes. Add small amount of broth to cornstarch and stir. Combine cornstarch mixture, broth, milk or cream, and add to scallions. Cook on High 2 minutes and stir well. Cook on High 3 minutes more and stir well. Taste for salt.

TIP
Sauce goes well with steamed vegetables.

龍虾醬

LOBSTER SAUCE WITH BLACK BEANS

Quantity: 1½ cups   Cooking time: 9½ minutes

2 teaspoons fermented, salted black beans
½ cup water
1 garlic clove, minced
4 teaspoons vegetable oil
¼ pound finely ground pork (about ½ cup)
2 scallions, chopped
1 tablespoon soy sauce
1 tablespoon dry sherry
1 tablespoon cornstarch mixed with ½ cup water
½ teaspoon sugar
2 eggs, slightly beaten

Put beans and water in heatproof 1-cup measure, heat on High ½ minute. Let stand 5 minutes, and drain. Chop beans coarsely, add garlic, and stir to form paste.

Add oil to large heatproof pie plate, cover with plastic wrap, heat on High 5 minutes. Add bean paste, pork, and mix well. Spread in even layer, leaving center open. Cook on High 1 minute.

Combine scallions, soy sauce, sherry, cornstarch mixture, and sugar. Mix with pork, cover with plastic wrap, cook on High 3 minutes, and stir. Add eggs and mix well. Heat of pork mixture is enough to cook eggs.

TIP

This sauce does not contain lobster. Rather it gets its name because it is a classic sauce for lobster as well as other shellfish and fish. It is sometimes called fish sauce, indicating its use with a variety of seafood.

海鮮蕃茄醬
HOISIN AND TOMATO SAUCE

Quantity: ½ cup   Cooking time: 4 minutes

4 teaspoons ketchup
1 tablespoon hoisin sauce
1 tablespoon soy sauce
1½ teaspoons cornstarch mixed with 4 tablespoons water
1 teaspoon dry sherry
1 teaspoon American chili sauce
½ teaspoon sugar
½ teaspoon vegetable oil

Mix all ingredients together in heatproof 2-cup measure, cook on High 2 minutes, and stir well. Cook on High 2 minutes more and stir well.

TIP

Good sauce for meats and noodles.

咖喱汁

CURRY SAUCE

Quantity: ½ cup　　　　　　　　　　　　　　　Cooking time: 4 minutes

2 teaspoons curry powder (Malaysian curry preferred)
2 teaspoons cornstarch
½ cup chicken broth, homemade or canned
1 tablespoon dry sherry
1 tablespoon vegetable oil
Salt to taste

Mix curry and cornstarch together in heatproof 2-cup measure. Add small amount of broth and stir. Add rest of broth, sherry, oil, and mix well. Cook on High 2 minutes and stir. Cook on High 2 minutes more and stir well. Taste for salt.

TIP
Sauce is good with beef and chicken.

鲜菇汁

MUSHROOM SAUCE

Quantity: 1 cup　　　　　　　　　　　　　　Cooking time: 10 minutes

4 to 6 dried Chinese mushrooms
2 cups water
8 to 9 fresh mushroom caps
1 teaspoon vegetable oil
1 thin slice ginger root, minced
2 teaspoons cornstarch mixed with ½ cup chicken broth, homemade
   or canned
1 teaspoon soy sauce

Rinse dried mushrooms in water, put in heatproof 1-quart measure with water, cover with plastic wrap, leaving small vent. Heat on

High 4 minutes. Let stand 5 minutes, and drain. Discard hard stems, cut in ¼-inch slices, and reserve.

Put fresh mushroom caps in heatproof pie plate, sprinkle with oil, and stir. Cook on High 1 minute. Add Chinese mushrooms and rest of ingredients. Mix well. Spread in even layer, leaving center open. Cook on High 3 minutes, and stir. Spread evenly, leaving center open. Cook on High 2 minutes, and stir.

TIPS

Always rinse dried mushrooms before soaking to remove small particles that can cause too much foaming when heated with water and result in overflow from bowl.

Chinese mushrooms can be left whole like the fresh mushrooms, if desired.

Serve on vegetables like cabbage and zucchini.

蘇 梅 醬

PLUM SAUCE (DUCK SAUCE)

Quantity: 1¼ cups   Cooking time: 3 minutes

1 cup damson plum preserves
¼ cup apricot preserves
2 tablespoons cider vinegar
¼ teaspoon salt
Dash hot red pepper (cayenne)

Put all ingredients in heatproof 1-quart measure and mix well. Place off center in oven, heat on High 2 minutes, and stir. Heat on High 1 minute and stir. Cool to room temperature. Sauce can be stored several weeks refrigerated in tightly capped container.

SOY BARBECUE SAUCE

Quantity: 1¼ cups   Cooking time: 5 minutes

2 thin slices ginger root, minced
4 tablespoons chopped scallions
4 tablespoons soy sauce
2 tablespoons sugar
1 tablespoon dark soy sauce
1 tablespoon dry sherry
1 tablespoon vegetable oil
1 teaspoon hoisin sauce
1 teaspoon cornstarch mixed with ½ cup chicken broth or water

Mix all ingredients together in small heatproof bowl. Cook on High 3 minutes and stir. Cook on High 2 minutes more. Stir well.

TIP
Use on spareribs and pork shoulder as barbecue sauce.

SWEET-AND-SOUR SAUCE

Quantity: 1¼ cups   Cooking time: 4 minutes

6 tablespoons sugar
¼ cup cider or white vinegar
1½ tablespoons cornstarch mixed with ½ cup water
1 tablespoon ketchup
1 tablespoon soy sauce
1 teaspoon salt

Combine all ingredients in small heatproof bowl. Cook on High 4 minutes. Stir well.

TIP
Serve on meats, fish, and vegetables. When used with vegetables, omit salt.

CHILI OIL

Quantity: ½ cup   Cooking time: 7 minutes

3 to 4 fresh hot red peppers
½ cup vegetable oil
2 teaspoons sesame oil

Remove stems of peppers and discard. Do not discard seeds. Chop peppers and seeds coarsely. Mix peppers with vegetable oil in heatproof 2-cup measure. Cover with plastic wrap, leaving small vent. Cook on High 2 minutes, stir, re-cover, and vent. Heat on Low 5 minutes, stir, and cool to room temperature. Pour off oil, discard peppers and seeds. Add sesame oil to pepper oil and stir well. Store in tightly capped container.

TIPS
A few drops of chili oil will add a hot spicy flavor to main dishes, dips, and sauces. Can be substituted for the flavor of hot chili paste.

Cooking seeds with peppers increases the hot flavor of the oil.

Homemade chili oil is more economical than the commercial product.

辣醬

SZECHUAN-STYLE CHILI PASTE

Quantity: ½ cup

Cooking time: 12 minutes

¼ pound hot red or green peppers
3 garlic cloves, minced
1 tablespoon soy sauce
1 tablespoon vegetable oil
½ teaspoon salt

Remove stems of peppers and discard. Do not discard seeds. Halve peppers lengthwise, then slice crosswise in 1-inch strips. Chop peppers and seeds to medium coarseness in food processor or blender. Put peppers and rest of ingredients in heatproof 2-cup measure. Mix well, and cover with plastic wrap. Cook on High 2 minutes, stir, and re-cover. Cook on Low 5 minutes, stir, and re-cover. Cook on Low 5 minutes more and stir. Cool to room temperature and store in tightly capped container.

TIPS
Cooking seeds with peppers increases hot flavor of the paste.

Homemade chili paste is more economical than the commercial product.

甜酸辣醬
HOT SWEET-AND-SOUR SAUCE

Quantity: 1 cup   Cooking time: 4 minutes

6 tablespoons sugar
4 tablespoons cider vinegar
2 tablespoons chopped scallions
4 teaspoons cornstarch mixed with ½ cup water
1 tablespoon soy sauce
1 teaspoon hot chili paste or ½ dried crushed red peppers or more to
taste
1 teaspoon sesame oil (optional)
2 thin slices ginger root, minced

Combine all ingredients in heatproof 1-quart measure. Cook on High 2 minutes and stir. Cook on High 2 minutes more and stir well.

TIP
This is a good sauce for pork, chicken, and seafood.

薑油
GINGER OIL

Quantity: 2 tablespoons   Cooking time: ½ minute

2 to 3 slices ginger root
2 tablespoons vegetable oil

Cut ginger root in ¼-inch-thick slices. Put ginger root and oil in heatproof 1-cup measure. Cover with plastic wrap, leaving small vent, and cook on High ½ minute. Cool to room temperature and remove ginger slices. Store in tightly capped container.

TIP
A few drops of ginger oil will add a spicy flavor to main dishes, dips, and sauces.

四川辣椒油
RED PEPPER OIL

Quantity: ½ cup   Cooking time: 2 minutes

2 tablespoons hot red pepper (cayenne)
½ cup vegetable oil

Mix pepper with oil in heatproof 1-cup measure. Cover with plastic wrap, leaving small vent. Cook on High 2 minutes, and stir. Cool to room temperature, pour off clear red oil. Discard pepper sediment. Store in tightly capped container.

TIPS
A few drops of pepper oil will add a hot spicy flavor to main dishes, dips, and sauces. Can be substituted for the flavor of hot chili paste.

Homemade red pepper oil is more economical than the commercial product.

生菜汁
SALAD DRESSING

Quantity: ¼ cup   Cooking time: 2½ minutes

1 tablespoon vegetable oil
1 thin slice ginger root, minced
¼ teaspoon hot red pepper (cayenne)
1 tablespoon soy sauce
1 tablespoon cider or white vinegar
½ teaspoon sesame oil (optional)
1½ teaspoons sugar
½ teaspoon salt
1 scallion, chopped

Mix oil, ginger, and pepper in heatproof 1-cup measure. Heat on High 2½ minutes. Add soy sauce, vinegar, sesame oil, sugar, salt, and stir. Add scallions and mix well. Dressing can be used hot or cold, and is excellent on cooked vegetables.

豆豉辣醬

SZECHUAN-STYLE CHILI PASTE WITH BLACK BEANS

Quantity: ½ cup   Cooking time: 12½ minutes

¼ pound hot red or green peppers
1 tablespoon fermented, salted black beans
½ cup water
3 garlic cloves, minced
2 tablespoons vegetable oil
1 tablespoon soy sauce

Remove stems of peppers and discard. Do not discard seeds. Halve peppers lengthwise, then slice crosswise in 1-inch strips. Chop peppers and seeds to medium coarseness in food processor or blender, and reserve.

Put beans and water in heatproof 1-cup measure. Heat on High ½ minute. Let stand 5 minutes, and drain. Chop coarsely.

Mix peppers, beans, and rest of ingredients in heatproof 2-cup measure, and cover with plastic wrap. Cook on High 2 minutes, stir, and re-cover. Cook on Low 5 minutes, stir, and re-cover. Cook on Low 5 minutes more and stir. Cool to room temperature and store in tightly capped container.

TIPS
Cooking seeds with peppers increases hot flavor of the paste.

Homemade chili paste is more economical than the commercial product.

五香粉
FIVE-SPICE POWDER

Quantity: 2½ ounces   Uncooked

1 tablespoon ground cinnamon
1 tablespoon ground cloves
1 tablespoon ground fennel
1 tablespoon ground star anise
1 tablespoon ground Szechuan peppercorns

Blend all ingredients together thoroughly. Store in tightly capped container.

TIPS

Ground anise seeds can be substituted for star anise. White pepper can be substituted for Szechuan pepper; both are mild peppers.

Homemade five-spice powder is more economical than the commercial product. All the ingredients are available in specialty stores or supermarkets.

11 · DESSERTS

The Chinese may serve a sweet dish like fruit soup during a meal for contrast but not as a final course. Pastries, candies, fruit, and nuts are eaten after meals and as snacks. Snow pears, grapes, peaches, plums, pomegranates, oranges, and watermelon, as well as several kinds of nuts grow abundantly in China. Candied fruits and nuts have been popular for centuries. As early as the seventh century, the Chinese refined sugar from sugar cane; an earlier sweetener was honey.

Special sweet cakes and pastries were associated with religious holidays and family celebrations like moon cakes on the Moon Festival, Eight Precious Rice on New Year's Eve, and sweet rice dumplings on Dragon Boat Day. In a charming old custom, prospective in-laws of the bride were presented honey-oil cakes to symbolize the forthcoming union of two distinct and different persons.

In this chapter, we have included six traditional sweet dishes: chilled fruit, fruit soup, candied nuts, rice pudding, stuffed dumplings, and rice gruel with fruit.

FRUIT SOUP

Servings: 4 to 6   Cooking time: 8 minutes

2 small cans mandarin oranges (about 11 ounces each)
1 cup water
¼ cup sugar
1 tablespoon cornstarch mixed with 3 tablespoons water

Mix together undrained oranges, water, and sugar in heatproof 1-quart bowl. Cover with plastic wrap, leaving small vent. Cook on High 3 minutes and give bowl a quarter turn. Cook on High 4 minutes or until just beginning to boil. Stir in cornstarch mixture, re-cover, and vent. Cook on High 1 minute more and stir. Serve warm or chilled.

TIP
Fruit soup can be served as a dessert or as a taste refresher between courses.

Fresh orange or tangerine sections can be substituted. If fresh fruit is used, add 1 more cup water or fruit juice.

SWEET CONGEE

Servings: 4 to 6   Cooking time: 27 minutes

¼ cup raw glutinous rice
4 cups water
⅓ cup raisins
⅓ cup chopped dried apricots
1 small piece dried tangerine peel (optional)
2 tablespoons brown sugar

Wash rice a few times with cold water and drain. Mix rice, water, raisins, apricots, and tangerine peel together in heatproof 2-quart bowl. Cover with plastic wrap, leaving small vent. Cook on High 8 minutes, stir, re-cover, and vent. Cook on High 4 minutes and stir. Cook, uncovered, on Low 5 minutes and stir. Cook, uncovered, on Low 10 minutes more and stir.

Stir in brown sugar and serve warm.

TIPS
Use caution when lifting cover to stir rice because of buildup of hot steam.

Congee is a rice gruel which can also be made with vegetables, meat, or fish and seasoned with a little soy sauce. Northerners serve this kind of congee for a light breakfast.

核 桃 糖
GLAZED WALNUTS

Servings: 4 to 6   Cooking time: 15 minutes

1 cup water
1½ cups walnut meats
½ cup commercial light sugar syrup
½ cup vegetable oil

Put water in heatproof 1-quart measure, cover with plastic wrap, leaving small vent. Heat on High 3 minutes or until boiling. Pour water over walnuts, let stand 2 minutes, and drain.

Pour syrup over walnuts, toss, and stir to coat. Spread nuts in single layer on waxed paper and let stand overnight.

Add oil to large shallow heatproof dish. Heat on High 10 minutes. Stir in walnuts, heat on High 1 minute, and stir. Heat on High 1 minute more, or until nuts are light golden brown. Do not over-brown.

Remove nuts with slotted spoon and blot with paper towels to remove excess oil. Let cool to room temperature and store in tightly capped container until served.

珠宝飯
JEWEL PUDDING

Servings: 4 to 6   Cooking time: 5 minutes

3 cups cooked glutinous rice (sweet rice)
1 teaspoon vegetable oil
½ teaspoon salt
4 cups water
2 tablespoons lard
3 tablespoons sugar
8 pitted dates, halved, or ¼ pound pitted dates, chopped
¼ cup candied fruit (cherries, halved; pineapple chunks)
9 ounces canned sweet red bean paste

Coat small heatproof bowl with oil, and arrange fruit in a pattern on bottom. Spoon half the cooked sweetened rice on top of fruit and smooth out in level layer to sides of bowl.

Spread bean paste over rice, leaving ½-inch margin from sides of bowl. Spread rest of rice over bean paste in smooth layer to sides of bowl. Cover with plastic wrap, leaving small vent, and cook on High 5 minutes.

Unmold by inverting bowl onto flat dish. Serve hot.

TIPS
Glutinous rice grains cling together enough to seal in the bean paste layer. Do not substitute short grain rice in this recipe.

Fruit pattern on bottom of bowl will stay in place if rice is very hot when spread.

Amounts of rice, fruit, and bean paste can be adjusted to taste.

Pudding can be prepared a day ahead of time, except for final cooking step, and refrigerated. Before serving, warm to room temperature, cover with platic wrap, leaving small vent. Cook on Low 5 minutes, then on High 2 minutes or until hot.

Jewel Pudding is a classic Chinese sweet dish.

元宵

STUFFED SWEET RICE FLOUR BALLS

Servings: 4 to 6   Cooking time: 14½ minutes

1 cup sweet rice flour
4¼ cups water
10 tablespoons canned sweet red bean paste
1 teaspoon salt

Sift flour and measure. Add ¼ cup water to heatproof 1-cup measure. Cover, leaving small vent, heat on High 1 minute, or just to boiling. Mix boiling water with flour, knead until smooth, about 20 times. Roll into cylinder and slice in 10 equal portions. On floured surface, roll each piece into a 2½-inch circle.

Put 1 tablespoon bean paste in center of circle, pinch edges together firmly, and roll into a ball.

Add salt and remaining water to heatproof dish (8 inches by 8 inches by 2 inches is convenient size). Cover with plastic wrap, leaving small vent, heat on High 8 to 10 minutes, or until boiling. Lower balls into water, spacing so they do not touch, re-cover, and vent. Cook on High 3½ minutes and remove from water. Serve hot with 2 tablespoons of cooking liquid added to the bowl.

TIP
Cover dough pieces with damp cloth while rolling out circles because dough dries out quickly.

杏仁豆腐
ALMOND FLOAT

Servings: 4 to 6   Cooking time: 3 minutes

2 tablespoons unflavored gelatin
5 cups plus 2 tablespoons water
½ cup plus 2 tablespoons sugar
1 cup milk, evaporated or homogenized
1 tablespoon plus ½ teaspoon almond extract
1 large can mandarin oranges
1 large can peeled, pitted lichees

Soften gelatin in 2 tablespoons water. Put 1 cup water in small deep heatproof bowl. Cover with plastic wrap, leaving small vent. Heat on High 3 minutes, or until boiling. Add gelatin mixture, ½ cup sugar, and stir until gelatin and sugar dissolve. Cool to room temperature.

Add milk and 1 tablespoon almond extract to gelatin mixture, and stir. Pour into pie plate and chill until firm.

Drain oranges and lichees, discard juices, and chill fruit.

Add remaining 2 tablespoons sugar and ½ teaspoon almond extract to remaining 4 cups water, stir, and chill.

Cut gelatin in ½-inch squares. Add gelatin, oranges, and lichees to chilled flavored water. Spoon fruit and gelatin into individual serving bowls, and add 2 to 3 tablespoons flavored water to each bowl.

TIPS
Almond Float is a classic sweet dish which can be prepared ahead of time and kept refrigerated.

Canned lichees are usually pitted. Fresh lichees are occasionally available and can be substituted. Peel thick reddish covering, remove large seed, and leave fruit whole.

12 · MENU AND PARTY SUGGESTIONS

A Chinese dinner has a selection of foods from four basic groups:
    meat dishes
    seafood dishes
    mixed vegetable and meat dishes
    vegetable dishes.
Boiled or fried rice is usually served with meals but may be replaced with noodles. Soup is served with meals, but Americans are accustomed to tea with meals. When you are planning a menu, your goal is complementary and contrasting flavors, textures, colors, and variety.

With Szechuan Pork, choose a simple stir-fried vegetable like Shimmery Bok Choy rather than highly seasoned Zucchini with Garlic.

Complement White Cut Chicken or Fish with Chinese Mushrooms with bright green Stir-Fried Broccoli or Stir-Fried Mixed Vegetables. Do not serve Red-cooked Duck and Soy Sauce Chicken at the same meal. There are two reasons: only one poultry dish is appropriate and both are dark-colored dishes. Similarly, you could serve Stuffed Mushrooms or Pork Shao Mai but not both with Stir-Fried Beef. With Lion's Head Dumplings you can serve a dark spicy vegetable like Garlic-Scented Eggplant. You can have texture contrast with Steamed Fish and Red-cooked Duck or Sesame Pork Tenderloin.

In this chapter we have outlined several menus for large and small dinners to show you the desired variety, balance, and quantities. You can plan dinner for two persons with two or three foods: a meat, fish, or egg dish, a compatible vegetable, and a side dish of rice or noodles. A dish from every one of the basic groups should not be included unless the dinner is for six or more persons.

While there are no rigid rules on quantities, a dinner for eight to twelve does not require eight to twelve dishes. Five or six dishes with rice and tea or wine are ample. With groups this large, we suggest you cook only one stir-fried dish because it will need last-minute attention. You may wish to add soup and a simple dessert. We suggest that you choose several dishes which can be partially or completely cooked ahead of time. You can heat them briefly on High just before serving. You can lighten your work at dinner time if you plan on one or two cold dishes you can prepare ahead of time. Both a rice and a noodle dish are appropriate for a large buffet. Soup is usually omitted for large groups because it is inconvenient to serve. For latecomers, you can reheat dishes briefly in the microwave oven.

The American custom most closely resembling dim sum (tea and snacks) is the cocktail party. You will find dim sum recipes for this kind of party in Chapter 1. In this group are several dishes that can also be served as main dishes: Bao Tze, Pearl Meatballs, Stuffed Mushrooms, and Shao Mai.

DINNER FOR TWO

**Lion's Head Dumplings
Carrots with Garlic and Black Beans
Fried Rice with Chinese Sausage
Tea**

•

DINNER FOR TWO

**Stuffed Cucumbers with Pork
Straw Mushrooms in Oyster Sauce
Long Grain or Short Grain Rice
Tea**

•

DINNER FOR FOUR

**Stuffed Chinese Mushrooms
Beef with Scallions
White Cut Chicken with Dip
Shimmery Bok Choy
Long Grain or Short Grain Rice
Tea**

•

DINNER FOR SIX

**Won Ton Soup (optional)
Curry Beef
Sweet-and-Sour Fish
Cold or Hot Chicken Salad
Stir-Fried Zucchini with Garlic
Jewel Pudding (optional)
Long Grain or Short Grain Rice
Tea**

DINNER FOR EIGHT TO TWELVE

Spinach and Tofu Soup (optional)
Beef Shao Mai
Sesame Pork Tenderloin
Spicy Steamed Clams or Mussels
Rolled Egg Dainties
Red-cooked Duck
Vegetarian's Delight
Almond Float (optional)
Long Grain or Short Grain Rice
Tea

•

BUFFET FOR TWENTY TO TWENTY-FOUR

Tea Eggs
Pork Bao Tze
Stuffed Shrimp
Oyster Sauce Beef
Soy Sauce Chicken
Pork with Hoisin Sauce
Tofu and Peanut Salad
Sweet-and-Sour Green Peppers with Walnuts
Noodles with Pork and Cabbage
Fried Rice with Ham
Dessert (optional)
Tea

13 · GUIDE FOR SUCCESSFUL MICROWAVE COOKING

This chapter contains alphabetically arranged explanations of the techniques used in microwave cooking and the terms in the recipes. When you follow these directions, you will have prepared traditional dishes in keeping with the high standards of Chinese cuisine. We have included a section on basic equipment and a table of measurements.

TECHNIQUES AND TERMS

Arrangement refers to where food is placed in a dish. In the microwave oven, food in the center cooks more slowly. When the food is dense or thick or has bones, leave a small center area free of food. This helps ensure even cooking. In our recipes, this is described as leaving the center open.

Cooking times should be followed carefully. Many brief cooking times are given in these recipes and most dishes should be served as soon as possible unless standing time is called for. We have determined by experiment the time for each dish because many factors influence the process. Dense solids like meat take longer to cook than light-textured solids like vegetables. However, one pound of meat does not necessarily take twice as long to cook as one-half pound of the same meat. Food shape is a factor since cubes take longer to cook than strips. Volumes of

141

liquids larger than one cup require much longer times to boil. We found that the addition of salt and oil reduces the time a little. Dish shape affects cooking, and food cooks more evenly in round dishes. With square and rectangular dishes, the food in the corners cooks more. Liquids heat faster in deep bowls than in shallow ones. Cooking times can change if large appliances—like washers, dryers, freezers, and air conditioners—are used on the same circuit at the same time as the microwave oven. If possible, use your oven on a separate circuit.

Cover, leaving small vent, means cover top of the dish with plastic wrap and fold back a small portion to allow some heat and steam to escape. This is preferable to piercing the wrap which may tear under the steam pressure.

Cover tightly means cover the top of the dish completely, sealing in the steam and heat. You can use glass covers if they fit snugly. Plastic wrap works well as a cover on any size dish.

Cutting:

Angle sliced means to cut food at an angle of about forty-five degrees and is used for fibrous and tough foods.

Chopped means to cut in small pieces not necessarily all the same shape.

Cubed means to cut in strips and then across into about one-inch-cubes.

Diced means to cut in strips and then across into small cubes; small dice are about one-quarter-inch cubes.

Minced means to cut in very small pieces.

Sliced means to cut straight across into thin strips, usually about one-eighth to one-quarter inch thick by about one and one-half inches long, and usually across the grain for more tenderness.

Slivered means to cut into very thin slices and lengthwise into very narrow widths or shreds about one to two and one-half inches long.

Density means how compact foods are. European chestnuts and carrots are dense, but foods like bean curd, water chestnuts, and mushrooms are not dense.

Dips are savory sauces served to enhance some dishes.

Filets are boneless, skinless fish slices.

Hardcooked refers to eggs cooked in the shell until the yolks are solid and the whites are firm but tender.

Marinate means mixing a sauce with food before cooking.

Quantities means the amounts specified in the recipes; larger quantities will not cook properly in the stated times. For larger amounts, cook more batches.

Servings in most of the recipes are planned for four to six portions to be served Chinese style with other dishes. See Chapter 12 on menus for more explanation.

Size and shape of foods should be kept fairly uniform whether you use slices, cubes, dice, or shreds to ensure more even cooking in the microwave oven. The appearance of the finished dish is important to Chinese cooking, and major ingredients should be about the same size and shape for this reason too.

Standing time means that food prepared in the microwave oven continues to cook for a short time after the oven shuts off because of absorbed energy still in the food. A few recipes call for standing time and you can leave the dish in the oven or remove it because only the food is hot, not the oven, unlike a conventional oven.

Stir-frying using the microwave recipes produces the same dishes as conventional methods.

Stirring and turning are ways to obtain evenly cooked food. The food farthest from the center and the top surface cooks faster because it receives the full energy of the microwaves and absorbs some. Less is carried to the underside and the center. Stirring exposes the underdone food. To stir, turn over and spoon or lift the less cooked food to the outside and push the cooked food to the center. With heat sensitive foods like eggs, the outer ring cooks almost completely while the center stays liquid. Rotating a dish a quarter circle turn, or ninety degrees, is another way to obtain even cooking. In our recipes, this is described as giving the dish a quarter turn.

Szechuan is a style of regional cooking characterized by mellow spiciness that can vary from mildly peppery to very hot seasoning.

Thawing or defrosting of frozen foods in the microwave oven preserves more texture and flavor than slow thawing. Consult your manufacturer's manual for directions.

EQUIPMENT

These recipes are designed for a standard microwave oven with 600–625 watts cooking power. The two settings used are High, full power, and Low or Defrost, 300–325 watts. These ovens are the most widely sold. For ovens of 400–425 watts cooking power, slightly longer cooking times may be necessary.

Heatproof glass cookware:

Bowls of one-, one-and-one-half, two-, three-, and four-quart capacity.

Measuring cups of one-, two-, and four-cup capacity.

Pie plates of eight-, nine-, ten-, and eleven-inch size.

Baking dishes of eight-by-eight inches and eight and three-fourth-by-thirteen inches size.

Ring mold with raised center spacer.

Covers.

Heatproof ceramic browning dishes have specially coated bottoms for rapid searing of small amounts of meat.

Plastic wrap used for covering dishes is available under several trade names.

CAUTION: Do not use metal cookware, metal trimmed glassware, or metal foil. These materials will seriously damage your oven.

MEASUREMENTS AND EQUIVALENTS

VOLUMES

		QUART	PINT	FLUID OUNCES	CUPS	TABLE-SPOONS	TEA-SPOONS	MILLI-LITER (ml)	DROPS
1 quart	=		2	32	4			946	
1 cup	=		½	8		16		237	
½ cup	=			4		8		118	
¼ cup	=			2		4		59	
⅛ cup	=			1		2		30	
1 tablespoon	=			½			3	15	
1 teaspoon	=			⅙		⅓		5	
½ teaspoon	=							2.5	
¼ teaspoon	=							1.2	
1 dash	=								2 to 4

WEIGHTS

		OUNCES BY WEIGHT	GRAMS (g)	GRAINS
1 pound	=	16	454	
½ pound	=	8	227	
¼ pound	=	4	113	
⅛ pound	=	2	56	
1 ounce	=		28	
½ ounce	=		14	
1 pinch	=			a few

MASTER LIST
OF INGREDIENTS

Anise, star: dried reddish brown star-shaped seeds. Store on shelf in tightly capped container; keeps indefinitely; licorice-flavored spice.

Asparagus: fresh green vegetable; peel stems of mature stalks.

Bamboo shoots: canned, unsalted; cream to tan chunky shoots; drain off liquid to store. Transfer to jar and cover with water, cap tightly and refrigerate. Replace water every few days; keeps 2 to 3 weeks; firm textured; bland flavor.

Bean curd: See Tofu.

Bean paste, sweet red: Chinese; canned; dark reddish paste. Transfer to jar and refrigerate. Keeps for months; sweet.

Beans, black: salted fermented; Chinese; soft processed soy beans; pungent aroma. Store in tightly capped jar and refrigerate; keep indefinitely; salty tangy seasoning. No substitute.

Bean sprouts: fresh or canned vegetable; cream to yellow color. Store fresh sprouts covered with water in refrigerator; change water every day or so. Drain canned sprouts, rinse, soak in cold water to crisp; crunchy texture, delicate bean flavor.

Beef, ground: fairly lean ground chuck or round.

Beef, steak: See recipes for recommended cuts.

Bok choy: Chinese; sometimes called white cabbage; fresh vegetable with green leaves and white branching stalks. Store in refrigerator; keeps 1 to 2 weeks; crunchy texture, delicate flavor.

Bread crumbs: dried, unflavored.

Broccoli: fresh green vegetable; peel stems.

Broth, beef: homemade stock and canned; latter tends to be salty, so when used reduce or omit salt.

Broth, chicken: homemade stock or canned; latter tends to be salty, so when used reduce or omit salt.

Cabbage, American: fresh, light green; round tightly headed vegetable; wrap snugly in plastic wrap, store in refrigerator. Keeps 2 to 3 weeks; remove core before using; firm crunchy texture, moderately strong flavor.

Cabbage, celery: Chinese; fresh green yellow vegetable with long stalks, closely headed. Store in refrigerator about 1 week; firm crunchy texture, delicate flavor.

Carrot: fresh; orange colored vegetable, called red turnip by Chinese. Fibrous crunchy texture, mild flavor.

Chestnuts, European: fresh nut; glossy dark brown soft shell with large yellowish kernel; usually imported from Spain or Italy. Store in refrigerator; keeps about three weeks; firm texture, nutty flavor. Also available dried in many Chinese markets; keeps indefinitely.

Chestnuts, water: Chinese; canned, peeled whitish fruit of aquatic plant. Drain off liquid to store, rinse in cold water, put in jar and cover with water; cap tightly and refrigerate. Replace water every few days; keeps about 2 to 3 weeks; crisp texture, bland flavor.

Chicken: fresh or frozen fowl. See recipes for recommended sizes and parts.

Chili sauce: American; bottled. Store refrigerated; keeps for several months; mildly spicy tomato base seasoning; condiment.

Chili sauce or paste, Szechuan: Chinese; bottled or canned dark red paste of chili peppers, fiery hot seasoning.

Chili sauce or paste with black beans, Szechuan: Chinese; same as above with black beans added. Once opened, keeps in refrigerator indefinitely; hot seasoning, use sparingly.

Clam: quahog or hard shell clam, fresh; grayish shell, yellowish tan flesh, slightly chewy texture, delicate flavor.

Corn, cream style: canned vegetable; delicate sweet flavor.

Cornstarch: white powder derived from corn; a thickener.

Curry: can or jar; yellowish powder, blend of several spices. Malaysian curry excellent; standard blend good. Keeps on shelf several months; mild to hot spice.

Duck Sauce: See Plum sauce.

Eggplant: fresh; shiny purple-skinned vegetable, firm to soft texture, delicate flavor.

Fish: fresh and frozen; cod, haddock, bass, whitefish selected in recipes for firm texture and delicate flavor.

Five-spice powder: Chinese; jar or homemade; brown powder, blended usually from anise, cinnamon, fennel, clove, and Szechuan brown pepper. Keeps on shelf indefinitely; fragrant.

Flour, sweet rice: Chinese, made from glutinous rice.

Garlic: fresh; bumpy round segmented white bulb, related to onion; cream colored cloves, strong flavor. No substitute. Garlic powder or garlic salt not acceptable.

Ginger root: fresh; brown knobby rhizome or root, yellowish flesh, usually peeled before use. Wrap snugly in plastic wrap unpeeled and store refrigerated 1 to 2 weeks; fibrous texture, tangy flavor. No substitute; powdered ginger not acceptable.

Hoisin sauce: Chinese; canned, reddish brown thin paste. Store in tightly capped glass jar; keeps indefinitely refrigerated; sweet spicy flavoring or condiment.

Ketchup (Catsup): American; bottled. Store refrigerated; keeps for several months. Mildly spicy tomato base condiment.

Lard: solid pork fat.

Lettuce, iceberg: fresh; light green vegetable, closely headed; crisp texture, bland flavor.

Lichees: Chinese; fresh and canned; reddish, pebbly skinned fruit with white translucent flesh and inedible large shiny brown seed. Canned fruit are peeled; soft tender texture; sweet delicate flavor.

Mushrooms: American; fresh, creamy white smooth fungi; keeps refrigerated from 4 to 5 days; tender texture, delicate flavor.

Mushrooms, dried black: Chinese; dried fungi; store on shelf indefinitely. Always soaked in water before use. Chewy texture; subtle delicate flavor. No substitute.

Mushrooms, straw: Chinese; canned; tan smooth hoodlike capped fungi. To store, drain off liquid, transfer to jar, cover with water, cap tightly and refrigerate. Keeps 2 to 3 days; tender texture, delicate flavor. No substitute.

Mushroom type—dried tree ears: Chinese; dried dark fungi; store on shelf indefinitely. Always soaked in water before use. Tender texture, delicate flavor. No substitute.

Mussel: fresh; ocean bivalve. Bluish black shell, pinkish yellow flesh; slightly chewy texture, fresh delicate flavor.

Mustard: can or jar; yellow powder, ground from seeds of mustard plant. Keeps on shelf indefinitely; mixed with water to make paste; hot pungent spice; condiment.

Noodles, cellophane: Chinese, also called bean threads; packaged dried. Very fine transparent noodles made from mung bean flour, in wiry threads wound in bundle; keeps on shelf indefinitely. Soaked in water before use; bland taste.

Noodles, dried: Chinese, packaged; fried dried egg noodles wound in loose mass; keeps on shelf indefinitely, bland taste.

Noodles, fresh: Chinese; packaged; wound in loose mass; uncooked egg noodle. Store refrigerated; keeps about 1 week, bland.

Oil, hot chili: Chinese; bottled; or homemade from hot red peppers, vegetable oil, and sesame oil; very hot condiment.

Oil, red pepper: Chinese; bottled; or homemade from cayenne pepper and vegetable oil; keeps indefinitely, hot condiment.

Oil, sesame: Chinese; bottled; medium brown colored oil made from sesame seeds; keeps on shelf several months; distinctive flavoring. No substitute.

Oil, vegetable: bottled and canned; light yellow oil; may be made from corn, peanuts, or soy beans. Keeps on shelf indefinitely, bland flavor.

Onion, green: See Scallion.

Onion, yellow: fresh; stronger flavor than scallion.

Oranges, Mandarin: Chinese; canned; bright orange fruit in segments; soft texture, delicate flavor.

Oysters, dried: Chinese; packaged; brownish, small shellfish. Keep on shelf in tightly capped container indefinitely; must be soaked before use; chewy texture, fish taste.

Oysters, fresh: ocean bivalves; gray irregular shells, grayish flesh, chewy texture; fresh delicate flavor.

Oyster sauce: Chinese; bottled. Dark brown liquid made from oysters and soy sauce. Keeps refrigerated indefinitely; salty delicate flavor.

Parsley, American: fresh; dark green vegetable with small curly edged leaves on branching sprigs; herb; delicate flavor.

Parsley, Chinese: coriander or cilantro; fresh green vegetable with small leaves on branching sprigs; herb. Tangy flavor, stronger and different than American parsley.

Pepper: fresh green or red vegetable; sweet pepper, crisp texture, fresh flavor.

Pepper, brown, Szechuan: Chinese; also called fagara; dried paired brown fruit of Chinese plant. Keeps indefinitely on shelf; spice. Mild seasoning. White pepper can be substituted.

Pepper, cayenne: red powder; canned; ground dried fruit of plant from the Capsicum pepper family. Keeps on shelf indefinitely; hot flavor; spice.

Pepper, chili: red powder or crushed flakes; canned; dried plant from Capsicum pepper family. Keeps on shelf indefinitely; very hot flavor; spice.

Pepper, hot: fresh, red or green vegetable of the Capsicum family; pungent and fiery hot taste; spice. Dried to make chili pepper.

Pepper, white: dried red berries of tropical vine, same as black pepper with outer coat removed before drying; used in light colored dishes and sauces. Keeps on shelf indefinitely; milder flavor than black pepper; spice.

Peppercorns, black: dried red berries of tropical vine. Keeps on shelf indefinitely; hot pungent flavor; spice.

Plum sauce: Chinese; also called duck sauce; bottled or homemade; dark reddish brown thick liquid made from plums and other fruits; sweet-sour flavor; condiment.

Pork: See recipes for recommended cuts.

Rice, glutinous: Chinese; packaged, dried; white grains smaller and rounder than other rices. Keeps on shelf indefinitely; soft moist texture; sticky after cooking; bland flavor. Used only for stuffings and desserts, never served with meals as regular rice.

Rice, long grain: packaged, dried; white long slender oval grains that have been polished to remove brown outer bran layer; soft firm, separate grains after cooking; bland flavor.

Rice, short grain: packaged, dried; white short oval grains that have been polished to remove brown outer bran layer; softer than long grain rice after cooking; bland flavor.

Sausage, Chinese: dried pork; dark reddish brown; steamed before use; chewy texture, spicy-sweet flavor.

Scallion: also called green onion and spring onion; fresh white bulb; green topped vegetable; firm texture, mild flavor.

Scallop: fresh; ocean bivalve, somewhat triangular and fluted shell, white firm flesh; tender, firm texture; delicate fresh, slightly sweet flavor.

Sesame seeds: dried; cream and black seeds from Africa and Asia, often toasted; crunchy texture, nutty flavor.

Sherry, dry: American; dry sherry is closest flavor to Chinese rice wine; common substitute in Chinese cooking.

Shrimp, dried: Chinese; packaged; brownish dried small shrimp. Keeps on shelf indefinitely; strong fishy flavor.

Shrimp, fresh: pink to green thin shelled; range in size from small to very large; firm, slightly chewy texture; delicate flavor.

Snow peas: also called pea pods; fresh; green vegetable, flat pods; crisp crunchy texture, delicate pea flavor.

Soy sauce, dark: Chinese; dark, almost black thickish liquid, extract of fermented soy beans with salt. wheat flour, and molasses added. Keeps on shelf indefinitely; rich salty flavor; used in special dishes.

Soy sauce, light: Japanese; bottled; dark brown liquid extract of fermented soy beans with salt and wheat flour added. Keeps on shelf indefinitely. Japanese soy sauce is best all purpose; less salty than light Chinese; rich salty taste; most common flavoring in Chinese cooking.

Sugar, brown: packaged; partially refined from sugar cane or sugar beets; sweet flavoring.

Sugar, white: packaged; refined from sugar cane or sugar beets; sweet flavoring.

Sweet rice flour: packaged; flour made from glutinous rice.

Tabasco sauce: bottled; trade name for sauce made from peppers of Capsicum family; hot pungent flavor.

Tofu: also called bean curd; Chinese; fresh soy bean cake, whitish, sold in cubes about 4 by 3¼ by 2 inches. Store covered with water refrigerated; replace water every few days. Keeps about 1 week; firm soft texture, bland flavor; absorbs other flavors.

Vinegar, cider: bottled; distilled from apples; acid taste; used as flavoring and as condiment.

Vinegar, white: bottled; distilled from grain; acid taste; used as flavoring and as condiment.

Whiskey: American; amber colored alcoholic distillate from grain; used as flavoring.

Wrappers, round: Chinese; packaged; cream colored; thin rounds of dough, about 2½-inch circles, made from wheat flour and water. Double wrap tightly and refrigerate a few days; may be frozen for several weeks. Wrappers used for Chiao Tze.

Wrappers, Won Ton: Chinese; packaged; cream colored; fairly thin small squares of dough, about 3 inches, made from wheat flour, egg, and water. Double wrap tightly and refrigerate a few days; may be frozen for several weeks. Wrappers used for Won Ton and Shao Mai. Thickness often varies; use thinner wrappers for Won Ton or roll out lightly; thicker wrappers can be used for Shao Mai.

INDEX

ABOUT THE AUTHORS

Lillian Chen spent her childhood in her native Peking, coming to the United States to attend college. She remained here to marry and raise four children. She earned degrees in home economics and dietetics and has taught Chinese cooking for the past ten years in Ann Arbor, Michigan, where she now lives with her husband, Kan. Her knowledge of the cuisine of China—supplemented by recent trips there and to Hong Kong to collect new recipes—combined with her experience as hostess and teacher, has enabled her to bring the wonders of Chinese eating to American kitchens and dining tables.

Edith Nobile is a New Englander with a special appreciation for good food from the world over. She has conducted workshops on the cuisines of China and Europe. Her background as a research chemist has given her the special knowledge necessary to develop microwave adaptations of traditional Chinese recipes. Two years of experimentation have resulted in the delicious range of recipes found in this book. She has three children and lives in Ann Arbor, Michigan, with her husband Vincent.